THE DESIGN DEVELOPMENT OF INDIAN ARCHITECTURE

THE DESIGN DEVELOPMENT OF INDIAN ARCHITECTURE

CLAUDE BATLEY

GYAN

Published by

Gyan Publishing House
5, Ansari Road
Daryaganj, New Delhi-110002
Phone: 011-47034999, 9811692060
E-mail: books@gyanbooks.com

Distribution Network
gyanbooks.com
India, USA, Canada, UK, Australia, France

ISBN : 978-81-212-3315-6 (PB)
First Published, 1954

2nd Impression 2020

Printed at: Gyan Press, Delhi.

The Design Development of Indian Architecture
Author: Claude Batley

THE DESIGN DEVELOPMENT
OF
INDIAN ARCHITECTURE

By
CLAUDE BATLEY, F.R.I.B.A.
PROFESSOR OF ARCHITECTURE
GOVERNMENT SCHOOL OF ART, BOMBAY

1954
D. B. TARAPOREVALA SONS & CO. LTD.
TREASURE HOUSE OF BOOKS,
210 HORNBY ROAD, FORT.,
BOMBAY, 1

BIBLIOGRAPHY

" Indian and Eastern Architecture," by James Fergusson.

" Rock-cut Temples around Bombay," by K. H. Vakil.

" History of Aryan Rule in India," by E. B. Havell.

" A Study of Indo-Aryan Civilization," by E. B. Havell.

" Agra and the Taj, Sikandra and Fatehpur Sikri," by E. B. Havell.

" Temples of Trichinopoly," by Major H. H. Cole, R.E.

" Indian Architecture " (3 vols.), by A. V. Thiagaraja Iyer.

" Dravidian Architecture," by Jouveau-Dubreuil, edited by S. Krishnaswami Aiyangar.

" L'Architecture l'Orient, Médièval et Moderne," by François Benoît.

" The Chalukyan Architecture of the Kanarese Districts," by Henry Cousens.

" Gwalior Fort Views " (local publication).

" The Architectural Antiquities of North Gujarat," by James Burgess.

" Muhammadan Architecture of Ahmedabad," Parts I and II, by James Burgess.

" Journal of Indian Art and Industry," by John Griffiths (School of Art, Bombay, 1894).

" Architecture of Bijapur," by Meadows Taylor and Jones.

" Bijapur and its Architectural Remains," by Henry Cousens.

" Moghul Architecture of Fatehpur Sikri" (2 vols.), by Edmund W. Smith.

" North-west Provinces and Oudh," by Edmund W. Smith.

" Town Planning in Ancient India," by E. B. Dutt.

" Indische Paläste und Wohnhäuser," by Oscar Reuther.

" Islamic Architecture," by Sattar Kheiri.

" Mohenjo-Daro and the Indus Civilization," by Sir John Marshall.

" Jaipur Portfolio of Architectural Details," by Colonel Sir Swinton Jacob.

FOREWORD

THE collection of measured drawings and details presented in this publication represents an endeavour to meet a need which everyone who has set out to study the elements of Indian Architecture must have felt. In the histories dealing with that subject, such as the excellent one written by Fergusson, the illustrations must need be small, while the plates contained in the various volumes published by the Archæological Survey Department of the Government of India, in the well-known Bijapur Portfolio and in other cognate works, are found to deal each with some particular locality or style, and many of them are, if obtainable at all, beyond the means of the average student of architecture. Again, they illustrate, for the most part, only the more monumental and ornate examples in the district with which they each deal, omitting all reference to its smaller domestic architecture, from which, perhaps, the most useful inspiration may be gleaned by architects in connection with their practice in the India of to-day.

Moreover, the works referred to naturally treat architecture rather from the archæological than from the architectural, or constructional, viewpoint.

There are, certainly, several works illustrating Indian Architecture by means of photographs, but, however good a photograph may be, it cannot take the place of a measured drawing for the student or architect.

The plates now presented have all been drawn by my Indian students, for the most part from measured drawings, prepared either by themselves or their fellow-students, while the remainder have been re-drawn in a somewhat more architectural manner, from various publications issued under the ægis of the Archæological Department of the Government of India, with the kind permission of Sir John Marshall, Kt., C.I.E., Litt.D., M.A., F.S.A., until recently Director-General of Archæology in India.

The origin of each measured drawing and the name of the delineator are to be found at the foot of each plate, and I take this opportunity of expressing my gratitude to all those who have thus made the production of the book possible, as well as to Mr. Robert W. Cable, F.R.I.B.A., and Mr. Alexander G. Bond, M.A. (Oxon.), F.R.I.B.A., for their kindness in reading the proofs and for other assistance rendered in connection with its publication.

CLAUDE BATLEY.

BOMBAY, 1934.

Descriptive Notes

Plate 1. HINDU PLANNING.

Diagrams A, B, and C indicate how the planning of Hindu temples develops from a simple octagonal unit enclosed in a square, the whole consisting of a roof supported by a group of twelve columns: to this other rectangles are added to increase the size and complexity of the building.

Diagrams D, E, and F show how, by a series of square and triangular slabs, which set the scale of the building, these octagonal units are ceiled and roofed.

Diagrams G and H indicate diagrammatically the development of the Indian spire, or sikhara, the most characteristic roof treatment over the square cella, or garbhagriha, of a Hindu temple.

The breaks in the external wall correspond to the internal niches, and as these are increased in number and richness, so the external breaks, with their multifold horizontal and vertical mouldings, each with its own respond in the roof treatment, grow in intricacy until the effect is of bewildering complexity which, however, on analysis, resolves itself back to the simple units illustrated in the diagrams.

Actual sikharas are illustrated in Plates 10, 11, and 12, the first two being from very simple examples, while Plate 12 is from a more complicated and rather debased late example.

Of the two actual temple plans illustrated in the plate, the first is the great Jain temple at Ranakpur, in Jodhpur State, and the other, also a Jain temple, is from Girnar on the West Coast of Gujarat; both show how the simple units of the diagrams can be developed until they form very large and complicated-looking plans.

Each of the five chief shrines at Ranakpur is roofed by a sikhara, as are the series of small niches, or cellæ, which group themselves just within the outer walls of the temple.

All three of the shrines at Girnar are finished with large sikharas. The central one contains the cross-legged figure of the Tirthankar within, while one of the side ones covers a pyramidal mass of masonry called a Somosan, representing Mount Meru, while within the other is a similar conventionalised representation of Mount Parasnath in Bengal, another of the many sacred hills of the Jains.

Plate 2. HINDU PLANNING.
A SOUTH INDIAN TEMPLE.

Jambuishuar Temple, on an island at the junction of the Kaveri and Kolerun Rivers, four miles north of Trichinopoly, belongs to the first half of the eighteenth century, although the inner portions are probably much earlier in date, the general development of such temples being that larger and higher Gopuras and surrounding walls are added, one after the other, at later dates, around the older and smaller ones towards the centre; thus the temple and the town around it grow outwards and increase in scale at each successive stage. It is quite possible that the innermost temple, or parts of it, date from the twelfth and thirteenth centuries.

The enclosures of this temple were subsequently used as walled encampments by Chanda Saheb, by the French, and also by the English and their Maratha Allies, under Lawrence, Clive, and Manakji.

TOWN PLAN OF JAIPUR.

This is a late example of traditional Indian town-planning and follows the rules of the old Hindu Silpa Sastras. It was designed by a Brahmin when, in 1728, the capital of the State was transferred from the old hill-fort palace at Amber.

The town plan, which is an example of the "Pastara" (couch) type, is characterised by the great circumambulatory road just inside the walls, by the "King's Road," running across the town from east to west, towards the centre of which the royal palace area faces. The town plan is then divided into seven nearly square and equal wards, by main cross streets. These wards are again subdivided severally into either four, nine, sixteen or, sometimes, sixty-four plots by other and narrower streets and lanes, according to the particular caste for which accommodation is required.

The plan in the case of Jaipur is not quite regular, owing to surrounding hills affecting the contours, but, in the main, the old precepts are followed with very successful effect.

The strictest control of the elevational treatment of the houses was exercised as regards height, fenestration, and even colour treatment, thus safeguarding the harmony and unity of the city as a whole.

Plate 3. MOHAMEDAN PLANNING.
KULBARGA MOSQUE.

Hasan Gunju, the Mohamedan servant of a Brahmin in the Delhi Court of Mohamed Tughlaq, after an adventurous career, established an independent kingdom at Kulbarga, in the Deccan, as the first of the Bahamani Dynasty, A.D. 1347-1435; this kingdom was not absorbed in the Moghul Empire until A.D. 1609. The mosque, which is raised on a high platform, is unique in having its whole area covered by a series of domes, the light being admitted only from the open sides. This form of mosque was not repeated, probably owing to the lack of privacy compared with the Mosque with its liwan set to the west of an open court with surrounding walls.

JAMI MASJID CHAMPANIR.

Mahmud of Ahmedabad transferred his capital to Champanir soon after A.D. 1484, and at once proceeded to build a very important mosque there, which is considered to be the climax of the beautiful Gujarat style; its detail most successfully combines the pointed arch with the traditional trabeated motif of the Hindus. The proportion of the liwan to the forecourt is very happy, as is also the lighting effect around the mihrab by means of double clearstory windows arranged below the main dome with its ribbed ceiling.

GOL GUMBAZ BIJAPUR.

Mahmud Abdul Shah, 1626-1656, as was the custom with Mohamedan kings, built his tomb during his lifetime, and certainly gained for it in size what he lost in its lack of grace and scale. The dome covers a clear floor area of 135 feet 5 inches, but, by the characteristic Bijapur device of interlacing arches, the lower internal diameter of the dome proper is reduced to 124 feet 5 inches, and its weight tends rather to bring the walls inwards than to thrust them outwards. The only reason for its having developed slight cracks is that wrought-iron bands were originally introduced in its construction and, now that the outside gilding has disappeared and the plaster below deteriorated, these ties are corroding.

TAJ MAHAL AND ITS GARDEN LAY-OUT.

One of the many charms of the Taj Mahal at Agra is its setting, the garden is completely walled, and, as one stands below the centre of the domed entrance gateway and looks northwards, its arched opening exactly frames the tomb at the end of the vista. The focal point of the central fountain, where the main axial water channels cross, is just sufficient to keep the eye at the right altitude, the small lateral garden houses at the extremities of the main cross paths and the enclosing walls help to preserve the sense of enclosure, as do the mosque to the west and its balancing Pilgrims' Rest-house to the east, each of which marks the termination of the lateral axis through the tomb chamber itself.

The four detached minarets, although somewhat poor in design, fulfil their purpose in assisting to control the composition and focus the eye on the main building.

The whole composition is a good example of grand-manner planning on a somewhat small scale, and the fact that such planning is certainly indigenous to India can be traced in the lay-out of the simplest temple, in the magnificent temple-town plans of South India, and in the various Indian mediæval town lay-outs as reflected in the design of such a comparatively modern Indian town as Jaipur, already illustrated.

EMPEROR SHAH JAHAN'S PALACE AT DELHI.

Shah Jahan's red palace, which Fergusson considered to have been the finest palace in the east, perhaps in the world, is an entirely walled palace-town, with its west, or Lahore, gate axial to the great processional road (the famous Chandni Chowk, moonlight square) leading across the great parade-ground to the Jami Masjid of the town of Shahjahanabad about a quarter of a mile away; the whole lay-out was designed in A.D. 1638, and completed about ten years later.

In the Fort the street leading from the gate eastward was bordered by shops. Other shops and small dwellings also lined the first cross street. Farther east one passed through the gateway of the palace proper, with its musicians' gallery above, into the great public courtyard, on the eastern side of which stood the great columned hall of public audience, with the famous peacock throne as its central feature. The throne room communicated on the east with a further smaller court, on the east of which was the private audience hall overlooking the river. To the north of this eastern portion of the palace were the private apartments of the Emperor, including the ladies' quarters, the Moghul garden, with its wonderful fountains and, later, the little Pearl Mosque, built by Aurangzeb, while to the south of the private audience hall were the offices and the quarters of the palace officials and guests. Most of the buildings on this side were cleared away for the erection of barracks before Lord Curzon's time. The original buildings were, probably, at that time in a very dilapidated condition, and their archæological value was therefore not realised.

Plate 4.

The Buddhist order illustrated is from the Karli Cave temple, near Poona, excavated probably about the beginning of the Christian era. Its Chaitya hall is the largest yet discovered in India.

The order is very simple, but the general character, as well as many of the details found in these cave-temples, survived throughout the history of Indian Architecture, in both its Hindu and Mohamedan phases.

It is to be noticed that the sculpture above the capital does not give the impression that it supports the entablature, but is in the nature of high-relief sculpture applied as pure ornament to the front only of the great square constructional dosseret block which rests on the capital proper.

Plate 5.

The Kailasa temple at Ellora ranks very high among the world's famous architectural remains. It is entirely monolithic, being hewn from the hillside by quarrying a courtyard, about 250 feet long by 150 feet wide and from 50 to 100 feet deep, around a central mass of rock, which was afterwards shaped into a free-standing double-storied temple, while the two vertical sides and the rear end of the quarry face were excavated to form a two-storied cloister, with numerous inter-connecting halls and shrines, their open façades looking on to the central temple itself, which is dedicated to Siva. The fourth or front side of the quarry became the entrance screen to the whole composition.

The column illustrated is typical of the beautifully designed ornament of the period; such motifs persisted throughout the later Hindu period all over India, and certainly influenced even the later Mohamedan work to a considerable extent.

The temple is attributed to King Krishna I, who reigned towards the end of the eighth century A.D.

Plate 6.

Vijayanagar, one of the great South India kingdoms, enjoyed its highest prosperity between the accession of Krishna Deva in 1508 and the death of Achutya Rayal in 1542. It was during the latter King's reign that the temple, from which the order illustrated in this plate is taken, was built.

It is dedicated to Vitoba, a local manifestation of Vishnu.

The temple, the plan of which is given to a small scale, is but one of a large group of temples within the same walled enclosure, entered from three Gopuras set at the centres of its north-east and west walls. Outside this enclosure wall is still another courtyard with its own wall and three gates, the largest leading into a wide processional road known as the Suliah Bazaar, with arcades on either side and a fine tank to the east, itself surrounded by further arcades. The whole of the work is in local granite.

In the order, which is characteristic of Southern Indian work, it is worth notice that the Yalis, or Griffins, and other figures are never given the work of supporting the main entablature, but are, as it were, merely attendant figures, guarding the temple, rather than Atlantes or Caryatides; they are certainly reminiscent of the great winged bulls of the Assyrian and the Osiris pillars of Egyptian architecture.

Plate 7.

This plate illustrates three other columns of the Chalukyan style, two from the temple at Bankapur, described in the next plate; in the second column the detail of the coffered and carved ceiling is indicated; the third column is from the temple of Madhukesvara, at Banavasi. This district was an important one in Buddhist times, and it is recorded that Asoka sent a deputation there in the eighteenth year of his reign. The town is mentioned by Ptolemy, and is said to have traded with Persia; the cosmopolitan nature of the district certainly influenced its architecture. In Chalukyan times the province is said to have had some 12,000 towns and villages within its borders.

PLATE 8. (See general note on Chalukyan architecture, Appendix A.)
This plate illustrates the characteristic order of the Chalukyan style, and is taken from the temple of Sambhulinga at Kundgol; the plinth wall, or podium, which flanks the approach steps and the raised bench around the porch so characteristic of almost all the Jaina and Hindu temples, are shown.
The chajja (weathershade), with its brackets and stoneties, follows very closely the timber origin of the feature.
The other details of a similar entablature from the temple at Bankapur show the development of such a chajja with the timber-like decoration on the soffit at the return of its external angle.
The temples are executed in dark grey stone with highly polished, sharp, clean-cut edges. The circular portions of the shafts were turned on a lathe; the little pipal-leaf decorations on the circular portions of these shafts were incised after the turning was completed instead of being raised, as they would be on rectangular features.
Bankapur was strong Jaina centre in A.D. 1055, and it is recorded that there were five Jaina colleges there. In many of the Chalukyan Hindu temples the Gaja Lakshmi of the Jains took her place among the Hindu deities.
The temple of Arvattukambhada (sixty columns, although there were originally only fifty-two) at Bankapur was dedicated to Siva; the temple of Sambulinga at Kundgol, where the work is very similar, was, on the other hand, dedicated to Vishnu. This again shows how, in the Chalukyan territory, the worship of the favourite deity of the South, Siva, and of the North, Vishnu, met on equal terms.

PLATE 9. THE GENERAL MOHAMEDAN ORDER (EARLY GUJARAT). (See general note on Ahmedabad Architecture, Appendix B.)
This sheet illustrates the proportions of the columns, chajjas, cornices, and clearstory columns met with in Gujarat, about 100 miles north of Bombay. The style represents the introduction of the Hindu elements into Mohamedan Architecture; the buildings are the outcome of instructions issued by the Mohamedan rulers or their mullahs, as interpreted and afterwards developed by the descendants of the older Hindu craftsmen.
The plate clearly indicates in detail the plan characteristic of almost all Northern Indian columns, with their square rebated corners which, under Indian sunshine, give a most effective play of light and shade, compared with which the circular column, even if fluted, is extremely dull. Almost invariably the lower line of the architrave beam is level with the lower line of the overhang of the chajja, or weathershade, and when, as usual, bracket-capitals shorten the span of the beam on three sides, the fourth, or front bracket, helps to support the overhanging chajji itself; this is as good an example of functional design as any of the Gothic builders could produce.
In the earlier Hindu styles the proportions of the orders and their subdivisions were governed by tabulated and memorised rules, but there appears to have been a refreshing freedom when practically the same craftsmen were engaged to build for their Mohamedan masters, with instructions based on but vaguely visualised Saracenic prototypes. The proportions of the columns then varied, as will be seen, from 9 to 12 diameters in height. In the earliest of the Ahmedabad mosques, the columns supporting the roof before the mihrab or praying niche reach from the floor to the top of the clearstory ceiling, and are sometimes as much as 24 diameters high, with rather painful effect; this disproportion was, however, soon realised by the Indian craftsmen and abandoned. It only prevailed while the craftsmen were experimenting with the new problem of harmonising the great arches of the façade screen (on the introduction of which their Mohamedan clients insisted), with the bracketed Hindu columns in the inner and flanking bays of the liwan. That they eventually solved so difficult a problem successfully and in so short a time redounds to their credit as architects.

PLATE 10.
This is a small temple at Trimbak, near the source of the sacred river Godaveri, and may be said to be typical of the simplest form of Hindu temple in the districts to the north of the Chalukyan areas.
The temple consists of a shrine (gabhara) covered by a Hindu steeple (sikhara), an enclosed prayer hall (mandapam), here reduced to a mere vestibule, and a pillared entrance porch, in this case roofed by a pyramidal roof.
The horizontality of the plinth and walls of the shrine and the verticality of the sikhara itself blend very harmoniously with the lighter construction of the porch, and together they emphasise the expression of purpose of the whole composition.
The cusped arches of the porch and the somewhat bulbous nature of the pilasters of the mandapam niches point to the influence of the Mohamedan Architecture of the then rulers of the district.

PLATE 11.
Water, very naturally, has always been held in great reverence by the inhabitants of India, for their very existence depends on the arrival of the rain-laden monsoon winds from the south-west, which occurs between the middle of May and the end of June each year.
These rain-clouds sweep over India during the three months following this date, being combed by the Western Ghats and held up and frozen by the Himalayas, when they swirl round and return, giving a somewhat less violent monsoon from the north-east, which more directly affects the eastern parts of the peninsula.
One of the most sacred rivers of India is the Godaveri, whose source is at Trimbak, a few miles from Nasik. The plate illustrates the Sacred Bathing Tank there: a renowned place of pilgrimage. The tank has enclosing walls and a colonnaded verandah on its west and on part of its north and south sides, the remainder having similar colonnades, but without the protecting wall. Towards the south-east corner is a little temple for the use of the devout bathers.
The temple is quite a typical one, but its plan is modified to suit its special purpose and position. Its little porch is covered by a low dome, its mandapam, or worship hall, by a pyramidal roof, and its shrine, or cella, by the typical sikhara or spire. The architecture is a happy combination of what is called the Indo-Aryan style and that of the Moghuls, probably in this case influenced by the Peshwas, who were at that time in possession of Nasik. The steps down to the tank allow it to be used at all seasons, both during the rains, when the monsoon waters fill it, and during the dry months that follow, when they gradually subside, by evaporation and leakage. It is likely that the date of this particular building is a little earlier than that of the temple illustrated in Plate 10, which stands but a few hundred yards away.

PLATE 12.
This is a portion of a very striking example of the persistent survival of Hindu forms till the end almost of the Moghul Empire; the general lines of the exterior are those of the earliest of the Chalukyan temple forms.
The wonderful horizontality and the deep mouldings point to the survival from even farther back of the influence of the monolithic cave architecture of ancient India. Here, however, such features contrast with the Moghul work of Akbar at Fatehpur Sikri, on which the interior of the temple is based. The portion illustrated is one of the double cellæ of the temple; they are approached from a long mandapam with a three-way porch. The contrast between interior and exterior here is as if a church had been designed in the eighteenth century with an early Gothic exterior and a late Renaissance interior.
The temple is at Brindaban, in the Muttra District, and is executed in red stone; it was built by Maharajah Man Singh of Amber (Jaipur), one of the allies of Akbar, towards the end of the sixteenth century.

PLATE 13. PLAN AND DETAIL OF THE PULPIT IN AHMED SHAH'S MOSQUE AT AHMEDABAD.
This is one of the oldest mosques in Ahmedabad, having been built about A.D. 1414; it is roofed by ten domes, with smaller ones between them, supported in all by 152 columns, of which details appear on the plate. Each is apparently composed of two columns taken from Hindu temples and superimposed, with a block inserted between them to give the required height. They are of white and red sandstone, except the two on either side of the mihrab (those on the left-hand side of the front elevation on the plate); these are of white marble, but have been designed to match the re-used ones. There is little doubt therefore that the typical Mohamedan column in Ahmedabad was of direct Hindu origin.
Most of the coursed dome stones of this mosque were also taken from desecrated Hindu temples, and thus again it is clear that the direct origin of the later mosque roofs is Hindu. The mimbar, or pulpit, is of white marble; the newels, with their characteristic bell and chain ornament, were probably taken direct from some Hindu temple.
It is the old story of the early Christian churches of Italy built from the spoils of the earlier pagan temples.

PLATE 14. THE NORTHERN BAY OF BAI-HARIR'S GARDEN MOSQUE AT ASARWA, AHMEDABAD. (See note on Plate 15).
This is the northernmost of the five bays of a little mosque built by Bai-Harir in her garden suburb about A.D. 1550. It exhibits a very typical form of dome construction, based on the old Hindu principle of oversailing horizontal courses; it also illustrates typical dome finial and parapet cresting.

PLATE 15. THE ENTRANCE CHATRI, OR PAVILION, TO BAI-HARIR'S WELL AT ASARWA, AHMEDABAD, BUILT ABOUT A.D. 1500.
Such large wells, or bauris, were a common feature in India both in Hindu and Mohamedan times; the length of the stepped incline, from the raised pavilion to the draw-well at the rear of the lowest rest-chamber around the octagonal main well itself, measures nearly 250 feet, the width of the stairs is about 18 feet, widening around the landings of the octagonal well shaft to 24 feet. The first rest-gallery is 11 feet, and the lowest, or fourth, about 45 feet below ground-level. The water now generally submerges the lowest gallery entirely. Around these galleries, overlooking the water and the beautifully enriched shaft of the main octagonal well, loungers could secure a cool retreat on the hottest of days. Circular staircases, in the thickness of the retaining walls, lead from one gallery to another.
This wonderful well was set in a walled fruit garden, to the west of which are situated a small mosque and tomb. They are said to have been built by the chief attendant of King Mahmud's harem, an illustrious and pious lady, and his personal adviser. She is also credited with having founded the suburbs of Asarwa, which arose around the well, mosque, and tomb.
The cost of the well, alone, has been estimated at about a lakh and a half of rupees (£10,000)

PLATE 16.
This plate illustrates a number of Indian Mohamedan mouldings with their enrichments. They are from Bai-Harir's tomb, near her well, on the outskirts of Ahmedabad; they indicate a mixture of Hindu and Mohamedan motifs. Examples A, B, and K are of almost purely Hindu origin.

PLATE 17. (See also General Note on the Architecture of Ahmedabad and Gujarat, Appendix B.)
Over this private chapel, with the little mausoleum built near it to the memory of her favourite son, by a loving mother, soon after her husband's death, hovers a romance which explains the peculiar charm of this group of buildings.
The little mosque so impressed Fergusson that he called it " the gem of Ahmedabad " and praised its " unity of design," and noted the fact that " every detail is designed for the place in which it is put and is appropriate to that place." He believed it to be a more perfect building than the Erechtheion at Athens, and ventured to say that there was not a Gothic chapel that would not look coarse and plain if placed side by side with it.
The story of its erection may be told shortly. The son, Abu Bakr Khan, had been guilty of a hair-brained love escapade, characteristic of irresponsible youth, which had, unfortunately for him, ended in his capture and a sound thrashing by the householder concerned. This so affected the humiliated father, King Mahomed Shah, that he ordered poison to be put into his son's wine. King Mahomed himself died in 1511, and the mother, having nursed her sorrow till then, built the tomb and mosque, which were completed about 1514. If such a memorial did not exhibit a feminine scale and a delicate application of ornament, its architect would have been to blame. The three mihrabs, of which the one illustrated is the central, are in marble, carved with very restrained delicacy. The tomb chamber stands immediately opposite the mosque, so that the erring son, with his face towards Mecca, might contemplate the loving devotion of his mother, and so regain, through her mediation, his, and perhaps his father's, entrance to the paradise from which they both ran the risk of being excluded by their foolish impulsiveness.
Surely, a monument of architectural expression of purpose worthy to compare with the Taj itself.

PLATE 18.
This is a window from Daya Halima's tomb at Ahmedabad. The pierced stone jali shows the influence of the earlier Hindu floral, as contrasted with the Mohamedan geometrical patterns, and again demonstrates the success of the Gujarati craftsmen in combining the motifs of the two into an harmonious whole.

PLATE 19.
Here again, in a doorway from the same building, only a few of the smaller details and the absence of figure sculpture suggest that it is anything but the normal entrance to a Hindu shrine.

Even the ardhachandra, or half-moon step, of the doorway, a feature entirely foreign to Saracenic architecture, has been borrowed.
The absorption of the style of the invaders into that of the conquered is here shown to have been as complete as possible.

PLATE 20.
This plate illustrates some common types of pierced jali window panels. Here again is a blending of Hindu and Mohamedan motifs. Such a panel as F might easily occur in a Hindu temple of two or three centuries earlier in date than either Rani Sipri's or Daya Halima's tombs, from which these examples are taken.

PLATE 21.
Tomb of Kale Shahid, in Sultan Ahmed's tomb chamber to the east of the Jami Masjid, at Ahmedabad. This white marble tomb is the reputed resting-place of one Kale Shahid, but, more probably, is that of a grandson of Ahmed Shah, the founder of the city; if so, its date would be about A.D. 1500.
That it is a man's tomb is certain from the steep pyramidal termination of the sarcophagus. The body of a Mohamedan is always buried so that as it lies on its right side it may face Mecca.

PLATE 22.
The plate illustrates the two most important of several tombs in a colonnaded courtyard, or marqud (sleeping-place). The lower tomb in the plate is in white marble, the upper one is in black marble, inlaid with mother-of-pearl. They are reputed to be the resting-places of Queen Mughali, wife of Mohamed Shah II, nicknamed the gold-giver, who reigned from A.D. 1443 to 1451, and of her sister Murki, the first wife of the Saint Shah Alam, who later married the Queen herself after she had poisoned her husband in A.D. 1451.
The flat termination of the tombs of the queens is noticeable in comparison with the steeper termination of those of their husbands.

PLATE 23. (See also the general note on Sarkhej, Appendix C.)
This is the central bay of the two-storied colonnade flanking the great tank at Sarkhej, built in golden-yellow sandstone, in the Ahmedabad manner. The main structural members are plain, the decoration being almost entirely restricted to the gallery parapets and the enriched bands of the crowning members of the plinths and chajjas.

PLATE 24.
The plate illustrates the sluices for the supply of the great tanks at Anhilwada Patan and Kankariya; it shows how much care was taken over features which are nowadays generally left to the whim and fancy of the engineer. That at Anhilwada is the earlier and plainer. The three circular channels pierce a plain wall with pillars behind to support the roadway across the channel; stone railings and two small charts and interest to the elevation of the sluice. Probably the plain margins of the openings and the buttresses were intended to be enriched, but were left unfinished.
The sluices at Kankariya are a little later in date and very richly treated, and the long channel connecting them with the supply grid is also carefully designed.
Similar sluices occur at Sarkhej. All three are in the immediate vicinity of Ahmedabad, and were built during the fifteenth century.

PLATE 25. (See general note on Ahmedabad, Appendix B.)
The work at Champanir can be said to follow the most fully developed work at Ahmedabad, for the Gujarat capital was not removed to Champanir until about A.D. 1500.
The Jami Masjid, or principal mosque, of the new capital was built by Mahmud Bigarah to commemorate his conquest of that city in 1484 and was finished in 1508. Almost every detail can be traced to Hindu, or Jain, origins, for by this time in Gujarat the Mohamedan features had been almost entirely absorbed in the old Hindu traditional forms.

PLATE 26. (See general note on Bijapur, Appendix D.)
The Mecca Mosque, Bijapur. As shown by the key plan, the plate illustrates only the mosque proper, which, in this case, is set within an enclosed platform, instead of, as usually, only forming the western feature of the enclosure.
The dome construction and the main cornice between the end pilasters of the façade and below the main chajja are markedly typical of the style.

PLATE 27.
Malika Jahan Begam's Mosque is similarly very typical of the Bijapur style; it was probably built in A.D. 1586 by Ibrahim II, in memory of his wife Malika Jahan, daughter of Qutb Shah.
A characteristic feature is the accentuation of the central arch of the mosque by a cusped contour.
The building is in the dark bluish, rather brittle, stone of the locality; the spandrels of the arches and the whole interior are treated with a thin coat of stucco, in which the delicate plaster decoration characteristic of the later Mohamedan work is incised.

PLATE 28.
The plate gives details of the main cornice from the mosque illustrated in Plate 27; it includes the plan looking up and showing the enrichment of the soffit. Between the brackets, suspended from the crown of the outer row of small cross brackets, some 3 feet 6 inches in front of the main wall face, hang small stone chains supporting a locket-like stone ornament. It is from these chains that the mosque has received its second name, the "Janjiri" mosque.

PLATE 29.
The Jod Gumbaz (twin domes), known also as the Two Sisters, stand within a few yards of one another, and on that account are a striking feature, even in a city of famous buildings. One rests on a square tomb chamber and the other on an octagonal one; the latter is the subject of this plate, and below it rest the bodies of the traitors, Khan Muhamad and his son, Khawas Khan.
Khan Muhamad deserted his master when the troops of Royal Delhi invested the city. Aurangzeb conquered the city, and when he fixed the tax to be raised annually by Bijapur and remitted to Delhi, he gave orders that one year's contribution should be devoted to the building of a tomb to the memory of Muhamad Khan and Khawas Khan, his son, who had been at first imprisoned at Bankapur and afterwards executed as a traitor to Bijapur.
The sister dome, raised over the square tomb chamber, is that of Abdul Razaq Qadir, Khawas's religious tutor.
Although so late in date, the octagonal tomb chamber is one of the richest in the city; its dome construction is characteristic of the fully developed dome construction peculiar to Bijapur. By a series of simple, although apparently intricate, intersecting vaults, the sixteen sided gallery is achieved and, partly resting on this, is the drum of the main dome, sixteen-sided and circular externally. On this drum is built the usual Bijapur dome, bulbous externally and saucer-like inside; above its internal elongated drum is another series of pendentives, bringing its dome to an almost circular shape. Compare with the plan of Gol Gumbaz, Plate 3.
The main tomb chamber is without the usual counterfeit tombs; rumour has it that these were ordered in white marble by Aurangzeb, but did not arrive before the dissolution of the Empire. It is possible that those lying in the lower rooms of the Asar Mahal at Bijapur were intended for this building. The real tombs are as usual in the basement, in this case not sunk, as usual, below the ground, but within the exceptionally high plinth platform.

PLATE 30.
One of the finest groups of buildings in Bijapur is that known as the Ibrahim Roza (garden), in which stand Ibrahim II's tomb and its attendant mosque.
The two buildings are raised on a large platform within a great square-walled enclosure; a tank and fountain lie between them, the mausoleum being to the east and the mosque to the west. The tomb chamber was built by Ibrahim for his queen, Taj Sultana, but actually he was the first to be buried therein.
The building of the group must have occupied most of Ibrahim II's reign, A.D. 1580-1626.
The plate illustrates one of the enriched balconies near the north-east corner of the mosque; the decorative minarets, double cornice, and supporting brackets are all characteristic of the fully developed Bijapur manner.

PLATE 31.
The Mehtar Mahal forms the little gatehouse of a mosque which legend has it was built by a sweeper, because he happened to be the first man seen by Ibrahim Adil Shah I when he awoke on a certain morning. In order to be cured of leprosy, the King had been directed by his astrologer to give away a large sum of money in this way, so that the recipient might spend it in building a mosque finer than any so far built in Bijapur. The sweeper took the money, and duly built the mosque and the little gatehouse near it. The stone used is a limestone from a quarry about 30 miles from Bijapur, which takes a much finer finish than the local trap of the immediate district. Even to-day the enrichments are as fine and sharp as on the day they were carved. It is a most ornate building, but of very small scale.
The plate shows the ceiling above the first-floor room of the gatehouse.

PLATE 32.
The plate shows another Bijapur ceiling, this time in plaster; it is from a small but highly enriched building known as the Chhota Asar (or small treasury).

PLATE 33.
This plate illustrates a characteristic incised plaster ornament from the tomb of Behram Khan Khana, outside Delhi. No part of the ornament is raised beyond the ordinary plaster face, the interstices are just sunk to a flat face about an eighth of an inch deep, as if pressed when the stucco was soft. The sunk portions are sometimes filled in with flat colours—bright reds, blues, or greens being favoured. Similar enrichments were common in Bijapur, and elsewhere, from the sixteenth century onwards.

PLATE 34.
This plate illustrates the plans of a very typical Southern Indian house at Madura. A street verandah leads through a passage into the main covered peristyle, or reception hall; a further lobby communicates with the more intimate part of the house, with its own court; beyond this again is a further open court, with the well in its centre, and cooking recesses around, each with clearstory ventilation above them.
On the first floor the ladies' bedrooms are provided; the staircases are so arranged that access may be gained to them either from the street vestibule or from the second court, without crossing the public reception room, which was for the use of the male members of the family and their friends. This may appear to be a large house, but this is an essential where, under the joint-family system of the Hindus, there may often be three generations of a family occupying the same house together.
The whole site is surrounded by a high and strong wall, with a large gateway to the rear courtyard, fitted with massive timber doors, sufficiently high to allow an elephant to pass, since ceremonial occasions sometimes demand their use.

PLATE 35.
This plate illustrates details of the house shown in Plate 34. The columns are typical domestic interpretations of the Southern Indian order, the bases are in granite, and the rest in teak; the shafts are bound with brass at their upper and lower extremities.
The heavy ledged door, with its brass work, is characteristic of the south.
The domestic work here, however, is far less ornate than that found in the northern part of the peninsula.

PLATE 36.
This Nasik house is typical of the Peshwa period. It is timber-framed, and stands on a cut-stone plinth; the walls between the timbers are filled with local red brickwork, the bricks being about $1\frac{1}{2}$ by 5 by $1\frac{1}{2}$ inches, generally plastered on both their faces, but sometimes left exposed, and with lacing courses set on edge or in herringbone fashion.
On the ground-floor was the shop, or office of the owner, with a verandah around the internal open courtyard (chowk); in the centre of such courtyards generally stands a little altar, on which grows the sacred tulsi plant carefully tended by the ladies of the house.
On the first floor, to the front, was the principal room of the house, with again a wide verandah around the courtyard. The second floor was similar, with recesses for the household gods on each side of a small ante-room leading to the ladies' sleeping-toom overlooking the street. The verandah around the courtyard in the case of such small houses was used as the sleeping-place for the male members of the family; in the larger houses, rooms for this purpose were provided opening on the sides of the galleries around the inner court.
The interest in these houses is focused on the rich wood carving of the street front and of the columns and brackets around the inner courtyard, the heavy brackets, supporting the overhanging galleries, being of very massive scantlings.
Most of the houses at Nasik date from about the seventeenth to eighteenth centuries, and are examples of a wonderfully interesting phase of Indian Architecture, the study of which has been sadly neglected.
It is hoped that the few plates in this series dealing with such domestic work may do something to attract discerning attention to this fast-disappearing treasury of the wood-craftsman's art.

PLATE 37.

The construction and handicraft in this door of a wealthy landowner's house in the small town of Wai, in the hills some 20 miles from Poona, again shows the Indian carpenter striving to be up to date, but loath to abandon his father's traditions. The little figure of Ganpati, the elephant-headed guardian of the gods and of household good fortune, sits, as he usually does, over the centre of the main entrance.

One has only to compare this work with the scantlings and details of Plate 36 to see how the sturdiness and conventions of mediævalism were gradually but yet surely lost in the newer ideas of greater economy of material and a more naturalistic and cheaper treatment of ornament. It is probably a hundred years later than the house illustrated in Plate 36.

PLATES 38 AND 39.

These plates illustrate a larger type of Hindu house. This house is known as Bhaskarrao Vithal's Wada, at Baroda, the capital of the Gaekwar's State.

It was built in A.D. 1808-9 by one, Babaji Appaji Fansi, the founder of the present Thokarate of Vithalgad, in Kathiawar.

Babaji was a younger brother of Raoji Appaji, who, as the Commander of the Gaekwar's forces, and with the help of the East India Company, made the Gaekwar independent of the Peshwa's control. Babaji Appaji distinguished himself by his efficient collection of the dues from the turbulent Kathiawari tributory chiefs, and was made Diwan of the Baroda State in consequence.

The present chief of Vithalgad is the fifth in descent from Babaji.

After passing through the main gate on the northern front of the site, a large open court-yard is entered, with private temple on its north, a guest reception hall on its west, and guest rooms at the extreme north-west angle of the site. On the west of the site were further quarters and stables.

On each side of the main house, of which details are given, are two small courts, each 58 × 88 feet, that to the east having the marriage ceremonial hall on its east, the gateway to this court being large enough for the elephants, used on ceremonial occasions, to pass through. On its north are quarters which were used as offices for clerks and rooms for the guards.

The ground-floor of the main house consists of two courts surrounded by verandahs and rooms, that to the north for the male members of the family and that to the south, which contains the sacred tulsi plant on its altar, for the female members.

The main building was, until recently, seven stories in height, a mark of great authority, for in old India the number of stories allowed was regulated, or zoned, according to the social position of the owner; the two uppermost have now been demolished, but are indicated on the drawing. The staircases are all within the walls, one leading down and connecting to the private temple by an underground passage and the others up to the more private rooms of the family; the head of the family occupied the topmost story.

The construction is of plastered brick, with heavy timber framework for the floors, for the internal verandahs and for the overhanging balconies, which occur on all four façades. The timber was obtained from the neighbouring forests and the bricks were locally made.

This house is comparable with some of the mediæval palaces of the Florentine nobles, or with the great family houses of the late Elizabethan period in England.

The details are somewhat similar to those shown in Plates 36, 37, 40, and 41.

PLATES 40 AND 41.

These are of details from another large house, the palace of the Chief of Bhor State, in the Poona district of the Bombay Presidency. This house is later in date, and here the details show the influence of the British occupation and how the European Renaissance forms were interpreted and blended by the Indian craftsmen with their own traditional work. It may be said with some truth to correspond to the English transitional work, especially the half-timbered work in the country districts, designed and carried out by village carpenter-craftsmen rather than by architects. Signs of the foreign influence are to be seen most plainly in the columns, their capitals and bases, and also in the design of the balustrades, and in the raising of the height of the handrail of the windows; in the latter case, the device of adding the two horizontal rails above the normal Indian height of the balustrade is clearly the reflection of a tendency to adopt the European chair, in place of the more comfortable Indian mattress and cushions placed on the floor itself.

PLATE 42.

This shows the general planning of a house in a town that has been called the Venice of India, and is fast regaining the position, as the popular resort, which it held under the Moghul Emperors, who often longed for the gardens of Kashmir when on their expeditions in the Indian plains.

Here the conditions are more akin to those of Europe, as is evidenced by the care with which the house is warmed by flues below the floors and in the walls, so that advantage might be taken of the surplus heat needed for heating the bath-water. This house stands on the steep river-bank, and has a high stone plinth; the superstructure is in timber and brick, and the roof is covered with bark shingles, on which earth is laid.

PLATE 43.

This plate gives larger details of the carved timber screens and ceilings from the house illustrated by Plate 42.

PLATE 44.

Raja Man Singh ruled in Gwalior from A.D. 1488 to 1516; he was a Gujari by caste and altogether a striking personality, and a great patron both of architecture and of music. His work at Gwalior is worthy of greater notice than it has yet received.

His great fortress palace stands on the high cliff-like hill overlooking the present city. Fergusson considered it the finest of the earlier Hindu palaces.

The plate shows details from one of the several rooms grouped around the two inner courts of his Man Mandir palace.

PLATE 45. (See general note on Fatehpur-Sikri, Appendix E.)

This illustrates the most important of the group of three pavilions connected with the Zenana section of Akbar's palace at Fatehpur-Sikri; it is known as Miriam's House. Miriam-ul-Zamani (Mary of the age) was the Hindu wife of Akbar and the mother of Jehangir, his successor.

The walls of the pavilion were originally covered with frescoes and gilding; it is therefore sometimes known as the Sonahra Makan (or Golden House).

It is probable that Akbar's wives were accommodated in a larger typically Hindu house, known as Jodh Bai's palace, and that one or other of them only occasionally occupied these smaller pavilions. Jodh Bai's palace contains a temple, ample sleeping and living accommodation, including baths and latrines and, moreover, communicated by passages and stairs with the other pavilions, with Akbar's own lodging, and with the tower and terraces overlooking the sports ground and lake to the north of the palace.

PLATE 46.

This plate illustrates the most interesting, perhaps, of the three palace pavilions at Fatehpur-Sikri. It was built in 1572, and is known as Raja Birbal's house, but probably, since it is in the Zenana section of the palace, it was the pavilion allocated to his daughter, who is reputed to have been one of Akbar's wives. Birbal himself was a Brahmin minstrel and jester, who was given the title of Raja on account of his influence with the Emperor; he subscribed to the religious views of his broadminded master, who called his own combination of the various creeds " the Divine faith."

The plan of the pavilion is unique, and provides two semi-detached and yet entirely separate suites of rooms, each communicating by a separate staircase in the thickness of the wall to an upper and more private room with its own open terrace, originally enclosed by a pierced stone screen.

The general composition, with its play of light and shade, makes it one of the most attractive architectural features of the city and one from which many treatments and details applicable, with little modification, to modern Indian architecture may be garnered. The treatment of the chajjas, with their parapets, and of the roofs and domes is simple but effective. It is built, like all the work at Fatepur-Sikri, in red sandstone.

PLATE 47.

This plate shows details of the red sandstone panelling to the walls of Raja Birbal's house. The patterns are similar to those used for the pierced stone jalis throughout India by the Mohamedans.

PLATE 48.

This plate illustrates a smaller ground-floor pavilion reputed to be that of Akbar's Turkish Sultana. It is chiefly remarkable for the finely carved enrichments, including conventionalised flowers, birds, and animals, that cover almost every inch of its wall surface. The ceiling and roofs are in sandstone, but their decoration closely follows a timber and tile motif. It is said that Chinese were employed on some of the wall carvings.

The pavilion has a covered way communicating with the Khwabgarh (Akbar's bedroom); steps also lead down to a Turkish bath below the main apartments and up to the roof of the Diwan-i-am, from which the princess could take the air unseen and watch the Durbar ceremonies which took place in the court below.

The columns of the pavilion verandahs were originally connected by pierced screens, affording privacy to the inner apartments.

PLATE 49.

Having abandoned Fatehpur-Sikri, Akbar set up his capital at Agra, and followed a similar style of building there using similar materials. His son Jehangir, during his comparatively short reign, carried on his father's tradition, although his mother and wife exerted a good deal of influence on the details. This feminine influence on the court was emphasised to a much greater extent during the reign of Shah Jahan, A.D. 1628-56, since that Emperor did not exert the close personal control that was characteristic of his grandfather, and the work during his reign illustrated the extravagance that marked the climax of the Moghul Empire White marble and gilding took the place of the local sandstone and the exquisite craftsman ship of the earlier period. The example illustrated is from the little gallery overlooking one of the small courts of the palace from which the royal ladies used to bargain with the merchants assembled in the court below, or sometimes, during the gay fêtes and masques held by the court, with the courtiers disguised as itinerant traders, when the fun of witty banter and of very personal sallies waxed fast and furious.

The whole gallery is in white marble, with enrichments picked out here and there with gold leaf. It is an example of the later and more restrained work executed in the palace during Shah Jahan's reign, when the Moghul court had reached the climax of that wealth and extravagance which heralded its rapid decay during the reign of the fanatical and reactionary Aurangzeb.

PLATE 50.

Near the close of the Moghul Dynasty, in the early eighteenth century, after Aurangzeb had struck the names of all Hindu craftsmen from his muster-rolls, much of the skilled labour that had been trained on the palace works of the Emperors Akbar and Shah Jahan dispersed, and many of the best of the craftsmen found occupation on the palaces of the Princes of Rajputana, who were at that time taking advantage of the weakening of the Delhi influence to assert their own independence and to build semi-fortified palaces in their own States. Among these was the Chief of Udaipur State, whose capital is surrounded by charming lake scenery.

Built of rough and, comparatively, thin slabs of sandstone, backed, in the thicker walls, by rubble or brickwork, and finished with the finest possible white plaster work, the palaces and water pavilions glistened in the sun, and were reflected in the waters of the lake. Their interiors were often richly inlaid with mirrored and coloured glass mosaic, and the exterior finials and enriched mouldings were often gilded or painted in bright colours; the whole effect, however, is neither bizarre nor trumpery, for the clear atmosphere and cloudless skies, whether under the strong sunshine or the bright moonlight, which for the most part prevail in that part of India, seem to allow contrasts which would clash in duller climates.

The contrast between such a building as that illustrated in this plate and those previously illustrated reflects those striking differences of local materials and climatic conditions that are continually met with in the sub-continent of India. Nasik and Poona, at high altitudes on the edge of the Western Ghats, with their well-wooded sides and their heavy rainfall, were far from the influence of the Moghul Empire. Fatehpur-Sikri, Agra, and Delhi, one after the other the centre of influence of the Moghul Court with their command of the best workmanship and fine red and white sandstone, blazing days and cold nights with little rain, were the centre of the civilisation of those days. Udaipur, in the highlands of Rajputana, with similar climate and, also, within reach of fairly good sandstone and limestone quarries, felt the influence of the court at Delhi and the fashions which that city set and diffused, but was not yet able to vie with the capital's lavish use of marble and precious stones; it was, however, anxious, as far as its means allowed, to ape the lavish effects which had so impressed its rulers when visiting the world-renowned court of the Moghul Emperors, and for this purpose made use of coloured glass and gilding. The gateway illustrated in the plate leads from one of the landing-places on the lakeside to the inner court of the Gan Ghore Ghat Palace.

PLATE 51.

This plate illustrates an entrance, with an arcaded gallery above it, from one of the larger houses of Udaipur city; here, in the introduction of the frieze ornamented with panels and console brackets, as well as in the treatment of the impost mouldings, the

European influence is beginning to tell, as it did, even more disastrously, at Lucknow and Oudh later on.
It may seem strange for such a plate to be labelled as Hindu, but, as it is in a Hindu State and from the house of a Hindu, it could hardly be described otherwise; besides, through all the vicissitudes of the Mohamedan and European invasions, the old Hindu bracket beam, verandah railing, and chajja have survived and, in the well-drawn tracery of the jali-work, there still remains a good deal of the spirit that inspired the craftsmen of ancient Karli and Ellora.

PLATE 52.
This plate illustrates two delightfully designed jalis from the Palace of Gan Ghore Ghat, on the Pichola Lake at Udaipur. The forms have become modernised, but they still exhibit the same spirit of freedom of line and happy proportion between solid and void that characterised the carvings of some of the Buddhist work executed more than two thousand years earlier.

APPENDIX A. GENERAL NOTE ON CHALUKYAN ARCHITECTURE (A.D. SIXTH AND FOURTEENTH CENTURIES) (SEE PLATES 7 AND 8)

The country held by the kings of the Chalukyan Dynasty embraced the southern portion of what is now the Bombay Presidency, as indicated in the key plan on Plate 7.
The first king probably made Badami his capital somewhere about A.D. 550.
The Chalukyans were worshippers of Vishnu. The temples at Pattadakal are, perhaps, the finest in the style.
Remains of the style are found in the northern parts of Mysore, the eastern parts of North Kanara, the whole of the Dharwar, Belgaum, the Bijapur districts, and the western and north-western parts of the Nizam's Dominion. By reason of their location, during their struggles for expansion they came into contact both with the northern and southern influences, and the characteristic features of their buildings may be said to be a combination of the building traditions of the Jains from the north and of the Dravidians from the south.
Their country was, moreover, overrun from time to time by the Rastrakutas who had hewn out the wonderful caves at Ellora, and lastly by the Mohamedans in about A.D. 1310.
The earliest buildings were in large blocks of the local sandstone, the later ones in a greenish or bluish-black schist in stones of smaller size. All their masonry was laid on level beds without cementing materials.
The general effect of the architecture is a combination of the horizontality of the Dravidian, or southern, style with the verticality of the Indo-Aryan of the north. The resulting style, if less attractive than either of the pure styles, is remarkable, especially in its later phases, for its lace-like carving, comparable with the richness of some of the flamboyant churches of Northern France.
The Chalukyan temples consist of a porch and shrine and, between them, either one or two Mandapams, or columned and domically roofed prayer-halls, each crowned by a great central stone finial forming a pendentive at the centre point of its ceiling. These domes are always built in horizontal oversailing courses and are never of arched construction.
A peculiar feature of the Chalukyan work is the turned shaft between the base and capital of the columns; each is always in a single stone, which seems to have set the scale of the temple building itself.

APPENDIX B. GENERAL NOTE ON THE ARCHITECTURE OF AHMEDABAD AND GUJARAT, WESTERN INDIA (SEE PLATES 9, 13-22 AND 25)

Ahmed Shah, the founder of Ahmedabad, reigned in Gujarat from A.D. 1410 to 1443. He was the grandson of Muzaffer Shah, who had, when Governor under the Delhi kings, assumed independence in A.D. 1396. This independence lasted until A.D. 1573, after which Gujarat reverted to the Moghul Empire, until the latter's disruption in 1757 brought about by the weakness of the later Moghul rulers and the depredations of the Marathas. At its zenith, the population of Ahmedabad is said to have reached 2,000,000. It is to-day a very prosperous city vying with Bombay for supremacy in the cotton industry, but the glory of the Mohamedans has departed, and the city's affairs are now mostly in the hands of rich Jain and Hindu merchants and mill-owners.
The builders of old Ahmedabad were local craftsmen, descendants of the Hindu or Jain ancestry, hence their art assumed a local character, influenced by the climate, which is generally without extremes either of heat or cold, wet or drought, and by the local materials. Most of the old work is in a golden yellow sandstone carried from the quarries, about 50 miles away, on camel back, and, in consequence, the architecture is of small scale. The local craftsmen, during a century of experiment, grew very expert in harmonising the trabeated style of the Hindus and Jains with the arcuated style of the Mohamedans. Their city is almost unique in affording exquisite examples of pure trabeated and pure arcuated buildings of equal merit and of contemporary date. The pierced jalis of the window-filling, both in geometrical and in conventionalised floral design, are second to none in India. A similar style prevailed throughout the Gujarat district, and was brought to its climax in Champanir, 80 miles south-east of Ahmedabad, which was made the capital in about A.D. 1500.

APPENDIX C. GENERAL NOTE ON SARKHEJ (SEE PLATES 23 AND 24)

Sarkhej is about 6 miles south-west of Ahmedabad, and owes its origin, like many famous places in India, to the settlement there of a recluse, noted for his piety. The saint, in this case, was a Mohamedan named Ganj Bakhish, related to the great Firoz Shah Tughlaq of Delhi. Having squandered his wealth in dissipation, he became the disciple of a Mohamedan saint at Jodhpur and, after the latter's death, came to Gujarat and helped Ahmed to lay out his new capital there, but, refusing all honours, he himself retired to the village of Sarkhej, where he died at the age of over one hundred.
Mohamed Shah began the erection there of a splendid tomb and mosque to the saint's memory, and these were completed by his son. Thereafter the place became a favourite retreat of the Ahmedabad King, Mohamed Bigarah, A.D. 1459-1511, who built a summer palace there, overlooking a great tank surrounded by double-storied loggias and, as the custom was, mausolea for himself and his family. The architecture is almost entirely of Hindu or Jain inspiration, the arch taking a very subordinate place in the design. The tank, which is over 800 by 700 feet in extent, is fed by a channel entering from the west of the mosque, while at the south-east corner provision is made for carrying off any surplus water. The sluices are interesting, since they are treated as an architectural opportunity rather than as merely an engineering necessity, although not so elaborately as those at Anhilwada Patan and Kankariya, also near Ahmedabad, which are illustrated in Plate 24.

APPENDIX D. GENERAL NOTE ON BIJAPUR (SEE PLATES 26 TO 32)

Bijapur lies to the south of the Bombay Presidency and to the north of the Chalukyan territory.
Yusaf Abdul Khan, having been smuggled out of Turkey, served the Kings of Bidar, and was ultimately appointed Governor of Bijapur. On the death of the Sultan Mahomed he gradually severed his connection with the Central Government and in A.D. 1489 declared his independence. His short reign was occupied by wars against the Portuguese, and the Hindu kingdom of Vijayanagar, as well as against the lieutenants of the Delhi Government.
The independence of Bijapur was short-lived, and its history is that of incessant wars, feuds, and faction brawls; it is all the more marvellous, therefore, how time was found for all the building work that was done within so short a period. One of the most successful of the Bijapur Kings was Ibrahim I, who reigned from 1534 to 1557, while his namesake, Ibrahim II, and his famous Queen, Chand Bibi, strengthened the city defences, and were responsible for most of its finest buildings; this king shared with Akbar a reputation for being exceptionally broadminded and tolerant towards the Hindu religion.
The kingdom ultimately fell under the influence of Shivaji, and, soon after his death in A.D. 1680, it again became a province of Delhi under Aurangzeb.

APPENDIX. E. GENERAL NOTE ON FATEHPUR-SIKRI (SEE PLATES 45-48)

This city was founded by Akbar in A.D. 1565. "Sikri" was the name of the original village; "Fatehput" means "victory town."
He abandoned it for Agra, about 20 miles to the north-east in A.D. 1572, possibly influenced by the whim of Sheikh Salim Chishti, a Mohamedan saint, who seventeen years before had been instrumental in getting him to found the city. The city was 6 miles in circuit, and defended on three sides by high embattled walls and, on the fourth, by a great artificial lake. Its most striking building is the great Buland Darwaza, or gate of victory, which forms the South Entrance to the Jami Mosque.
The palace proper consists of many individually interesting buildings, grouped on the highest part of the central ridge around the Diwan-i-Khas, or private audience chamber, the official buildings generally towards the east and the Zenana buildings towards the west. The Great Mosque and Karavan-sarai (hotel) are some distance from the Palace and still further towards the west.
It is probable that most of the town itself lay to the west of the great mosque, between it and the Tehra Gate; why Tehra (thirteen) is applied to this gate is not clear, as it is generally believed that there were only nine gates to the city.
The whole of the buildings are of fine-grained pink sandstone from the neighbouring quarries; the ornaments and mouldings are almost as clean and sharp to-day as they were on the day they were carved.
The buildings exhibit Akbar's catholic taste, many being definitely Hindu, in conception as well as in detail. English Elizabeth and Moghul Akbar were contemporaries in date and, somehow, the spirit of the work carried out under their personal influence has a curious analogy, which seems to carry architectural expression into an almost personal psychological field; it is a sympathy which can be felt rather than explained, even when one endeavours to get at the inner meaning of their respective work, separated as it is by so many seas leagues. A similar parallel may be felt to exist between the later work of Shah Jahan and that of the French Court of about the middle of the seventeenth century.

INDEX

PLATE

Agra:
- Arcaded gallery 40
- Taj Mahal 3

Ahmedabad:
- Doorway, Daya Halima's Tomb 19
- Jali, Daya Halima's Tomb 20
- Juma Masjid 9
- Mosque at Asarwa 14
- Pulpit, Ahmed Shah's Mosque 13
- Rani Sipri's Masjid . . . . . 9 and 17
- Sluices 24
- Tombs . . . . 21 and 22
- Well at Asarwa 15
- Window, Daya Halima's Tomb 18

Arcade:
- Agra 49
- Ahmedabad 23
- Bijapur . . . . 26 and 27
- Gwalior 44
- Trimbak 11
- Udaipur 50

Arch 18, 23, 27, 29, 40, 41, 44, 49

Ardhachandra (half-moon); the semicircular projecting step before the entrance doorway to a shrine 19

Balcony 12, 23, 25, 30, 36, 49, 50, 51

Banavasi, Column from 7

Bankapur . . . . 7 and 8

Baroda, Bhaskarrao Vithal's house at . 38 and 39

Bauri, a large well with steps and underground resting recesses around its shaft (*see* Well).

Bases . . 4, 5, 6, 7, 9, 13, 14, 15, 31, 35, 40, 41, 44

Bathing-place at Trimbak 11

Bhor, *see* Poona

Bijapur:
- Balcony, Ibrahim's mosque 30
- Ceilings . . . . 31 and 32
- Malika Jahan's mosque . . . . 27 and 28
- Mecca mosque 26
- Two Sisters' domes 29

Brackets 9, 12, 13, 14, 18, 25, 26, 28, 29, 30, 35, 36, 40, 41, 45, 48, 51

Brindaban, near Muttra, Temple 12

Buddhist, Columns at Karli, Bombay Presidency 4

Capitals 4, 5, 6, 7, 8, 9, 13, 14, 15, 24, 25, 31, 35, 36, 41, 44, 49

Ceilings in:
- Ahmedabad 13
- Bijapur 31
- Fatehpur-Sikri 48
- Kashmir 43

Chajja (weathershade) 6, 8, 9, 12, 14, 15, 19, 23, 25, 27, 28, 29, 35, 45, 48, 49

Chalukyan (central Indian style) . . . 7 and 8

Champanir:
- Balcony at 25
- Mosque at 3

Chatri (Pavilion) 15, 24, 45, 50

Chowk (open court) 1, 34, 36, 38, 42

City:
- Delhi palace 3
- Jaipur 3

Colonnade 23

Column 4, 5, 6, 7, 9, 13, 14, 15, 23, 24, 25, 31, 35, 36, 40, 41, 48, 49

PLATE

Delhi, palace at 3
- Tomb at 33

Dome 12, 14, 15, 26, 27, 29

Domestic Work, *see* House, etc.

Door 35, 37, 40, 41, 43

Door-knob 35, 37

Doorway 19, 44, 51

Dravidian (South Indian style) 6

Eaves-Board 40, 48

Ellora, column from 5

Enrichment of:
- Balcony, etc., Brindaban 12
- Base 44
- Brackets . . 12, 25, 26, 28, 30, 36, 40, 45 and 48
- Buttress 24
- Ceilings . (stone) 31, (plaster) 33, (wood) 32 and 43
- Chajjas . . . . 28 and 48
- Columns . . . . 5, 24 and 48
- Cornices . . . . . 8, 9, 14, 16, 28 and 44
- Doors . . . . 37 and 43
- Doorways . . . . 17, 19 and 44
- Finial 12
- Mouldings . . . . 10, 14 and 16
- Niche (Mihrab) 17
- Panelling . . . . 20 and 49
- Parapets . . . . . 9, 10, 14, 16, 27 and 30
- Plinths . . . . 10 and 11
- Screen 43
- Shaft, Ellora 5
- Stone surface . . . . 47 and 48
- Tombs . . . . 21 and 22
- Wall surface . . . . 18 and 44
- Window 18

Entablature 4, 8, 9, 15, 23, 24

Fatehpur-Sikri, Pavilions at 45, 46, 48

Finial (Kalasha) 10, 11, 12, 13, 14, 30

Gabhara, *see* Shrine

Gallery (overhanging) 36, 41
- „ (arcaded) 49

Garden at:
- Agra 3
- Delhi 3

Gateway at Udaipur 50

Ghat, *see* Bathing-place

Goakh, *see* Niche

Gopuram (temple gateway) at Trichinopoly . 2

Gwalior, Man Mandin Palace at 44

Hip of Chajja 8

House at:
- Baroda, Central India . . . . 38 and 39
- Kashmir, North India . . . . 42 and 43
- Madura, South India . . . . 34 and 35
- Nasik, Central India 36

Inlay:
- Marble, black and white, Ahmedabad . . 22

Jain Temple at:
- Girnar 1
- Ranakpur 1

Jaipur, Town-plan of 2

PLATE

JALI (perforated stone screen or windows) 18, 20, 23, 40, 43, 44, 47 (ceiling), 49, 50, 51, 52

KARLI, Column from . . . 4
KASHMIR, House at . . . 42 and 43
KING'S TOMB, Ahmedabad . . . 21
KULBARGA, Mosque at . . . 3
KUNDGOL, Chajja from . . . 8

LIWAN, the covered portion, or prayer hall, of an Indian Mosque, *see* MOSQUE

MADRAS, Temple in Presidency of . . . 2
MADURA, Rajaram Rao's House . . . 34 and 35
MANDAPAM (columned hall for prayer or shelter) at:
Trichinopoly . . . 2
Trimbak . . . 10
MASJID, *see* MOSQUE
MIHRAB (sacred recess in west wall of an Indian Mosque), *see* NICHE
MIMBAR, *see* PULPIT
MINARET (small tower, or pinnacle) . . . 27, 29, 30
MOSQUE . . . 3, 9, 13, 14, 25, 26, 27, 28
MOULDINGS . . . 16

NANDI (Shiva's sacred bull) . . . 10
NASIK. Bathing-place . . . 11
Jathar's Wada . . . 36
Temple . . . 10
NEWEL . . . 13
NICHE, GOAKH (Hindu) . . . 10
MIHRAB (Mohamedan) . . . 17
ORDER:
Ancient Hindu . . . 5
Buddhist . . . 4
Chalukyan . . . 7 and 8
Dravidian . . . 6
Indo-Mohamedan . . . 9, 15, 23, 25

PALACE AT DELHI . . . 3
PANELLING (stone perforation) 20, (ceilings) 31, 32, (wood railing) 40, (wood screen) 43, (stone surface) 47, 51
PARAPET FROM:
Ahmedabad . . . 9
Bankapur . . . 8
Bijapur . . . 27 and 30
Champanir . . . 25
Trimbak, Nasik . . . 10
Udaipur . . . 50 and 51
Vijayanagar . . . 6
PAVILION (*see also* CHATRI) . . . 45, 46, 48
PLANNING:
Bathing-place. Trimbak, Nasik . . . 11
Chatri. Asarwa, Ahmedabad . . . 15
Garden. Taj Mahal, Agra . . . 3
Houses. Baroda . . . 38
Madura . . . 34
Nasik . . . 36
Srinagar, Kashmir . . . 42
Mosques. Ahmedabad . . . 13 and 14
Bijapur . . . 26 and 27
Champanir . . . 3
Kulbarga . . . 3
Palace. Delhi . . . 3
Palace Pavilions, Fatehpur-Sikri . . . 45, 46 and 48
Sluice, Ahmedabad . . . 24
Temples. (Jain) Girnar and Ranakpur . . . 1
(Hindu) Brindaban . . . 12
Trichinopoly . . . 2
Vijayanagar . . . 6
Tomb Chambers. Agra . . . 3
Bijapur . . . 3 and 29
Town. Jaipur, Rajputana . . . 2

PLINTH FROM: PLATE
Bankpur . . . 8
Brindaban . . . 12
Trimbak . . . 10 and 11
Vijayanagar . . . 6
POONA, Chief of Bhor's Palace, near . . . 40 and 41
PORCH, Trimbak Temple . . . 10
PULPIT (Mimbar) . . . 13

QUEENS' TOMBS, Ahmedabad . . . 22

RAILING . . . 13, 24, 36, 40, 41, 49
ROOFS . . . 48

SARKHEJ, Colonnade . . . 23
SCREEN . . . 43
SHRINE (Gabhara) . . . 10 and 12
SIKHARA, *see* SPIRE
SLUICE . . . 24
SOFFITS . . . 7, 44, 48
SPIRE (SIKHARA)
Spire, diagram of . . . 1
Trimbak, Temple near Nasik . . . 10
Trimbak, Bathing-place . . . 11
SRINAGAR, Radha Krishna Kand's House . . . 42 and 43
STAIRS . . . 13, 34, 45, 46
STAMBHA (pillar), *see* COLUMN
STEPS . . . 11, 13, 15, 23, 36

TAJ MAHAL, Agra . . . 3
TEMPLE:
At Brindaban (late Chalukyan) . . . 12
At Girnar, Gujarat (Jain) . . . 1
At Ranakpur, Jodhpur (Jain) . . . 1
At Trimbak, near Nasik (Indo-Aryan) . . . 10
At Vijayanagar (Dravidian) . . . 6
Near Trichinopoly (Dravidian) . . . 2
TIMBER CONSTRUCTION . . . 34, 35, 36, 39, 40, 43
TIRTHANKAR (Jain), the incarnations of the Holy Teacher of the Jains, thirteen have occurred and another twelve are to come . . . 1
TOMBS AT:
Agra . . . 3
Ahmedabad . . . 21 and 22
Bijapur . . . 3 and 29
TOWN-PLANNING AT:
Delhi . . . 3
Jaipur . . . 2
TRICHINOPOLY, Temple near . . . 3
TRIMBAK, near Nasik:
Bathing-place at . . . 11
Temple at . . . 10
TYMPANUM . . . 44

UDAIPUR:
Balcony, Dalpar Singh's House . . . 51
Doorway, Dalpar Singh's House . . . 51
Gateway, Gan Ghore Ghat Palace . . . 50
Jali, Gan Ghore Ghat Palace . . . 52

VAULT . . . 13, 26, 29
VAULTING (below dome) . . . 26, 29
VERANDAH . . . 11, 40, 45, 48
VIJAYANAGAR, Temple and details from . . . 6

WAL. Sirdar Raste's Wada . . . 37
WATER, dams . . . 24
WELL . . . 15
WINDOW . . . 18, 41

YALI, sculptured guardian-figures of horses, lions, etc., before the columns of South Indian Temples . . . 6

HINDU PLANNING

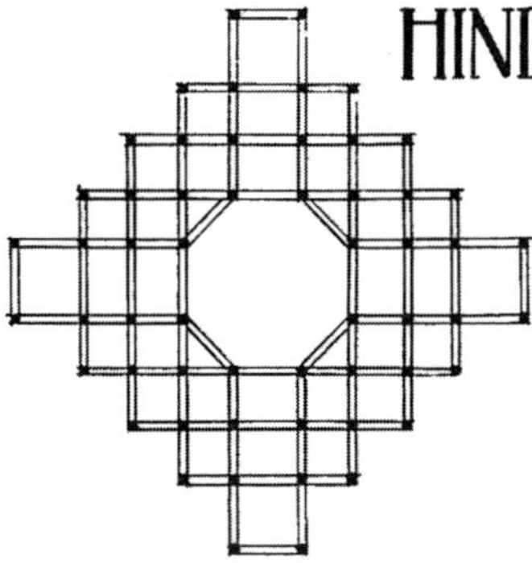

DIAGRAM C

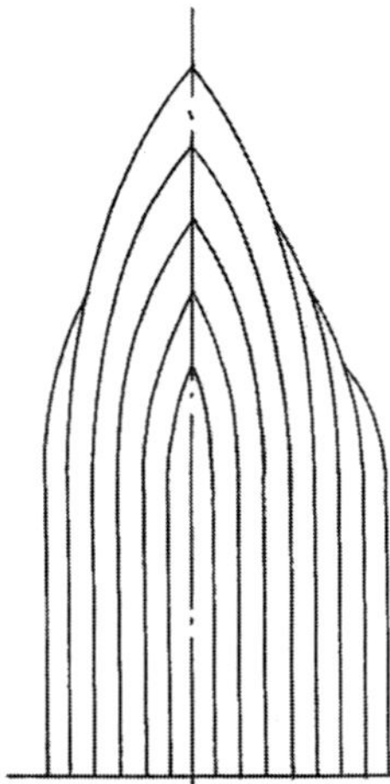

DIAGRAM H

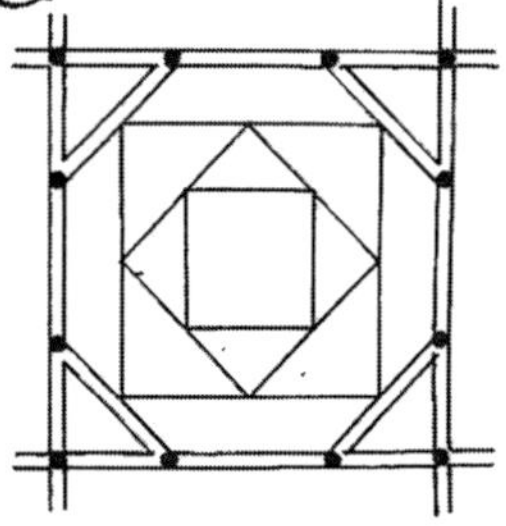

DIAGRAM F

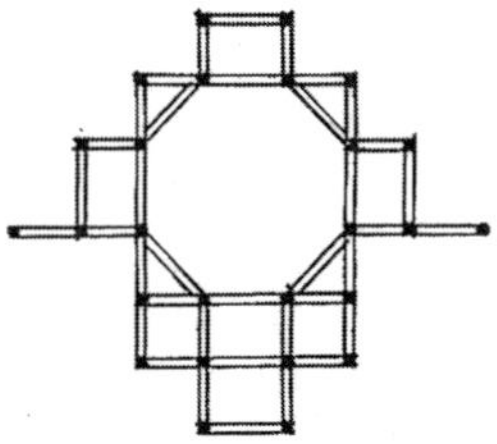

DIAGRAM B

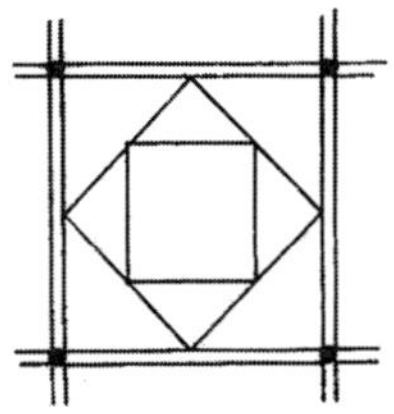

DIAGRAM E

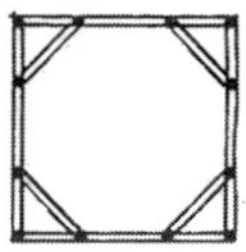

DIAGRAM A

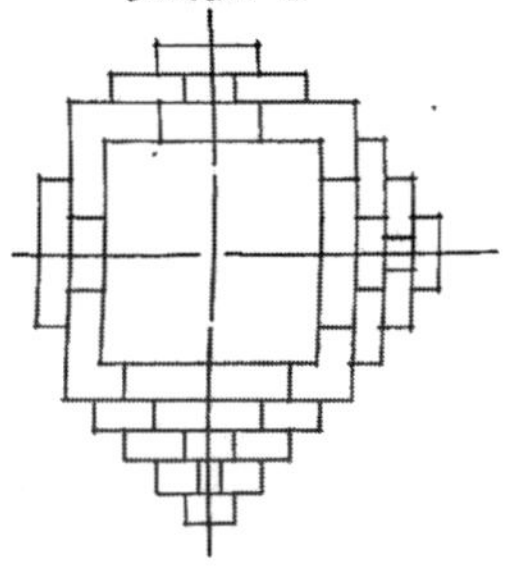

DIAGRAM G

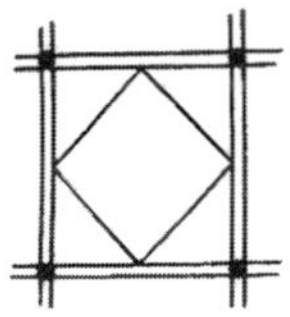

DIAGRAM D.

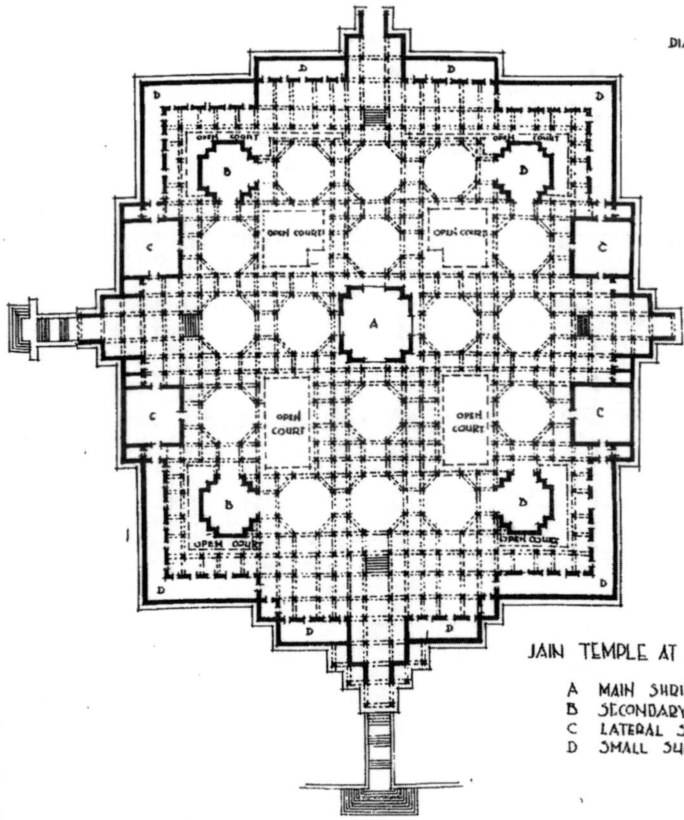

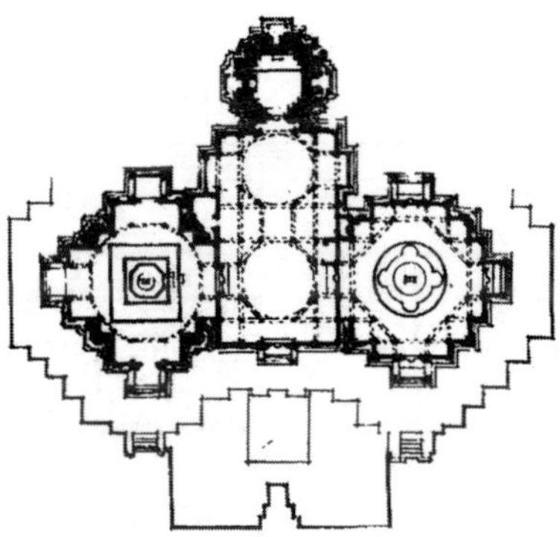

PLAN OF TEMPLE OF TEJPALA AND VASTUPALA.

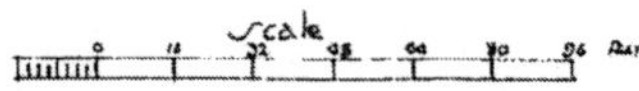

JAIN TEMPLE AT RANAKPUR

A MAIN SHRINE
B SECONDARY FOUR SHRINES
C LATERAL SHRINES
D SMALL SUBSIDARY SHRINES

DELT. L.K. NANDWANA

PLATE 2

HINDU PLANNING

JAMBUISHUAR TEMPLE, TRICHINOPOLY, AND JAIPUR CITY.

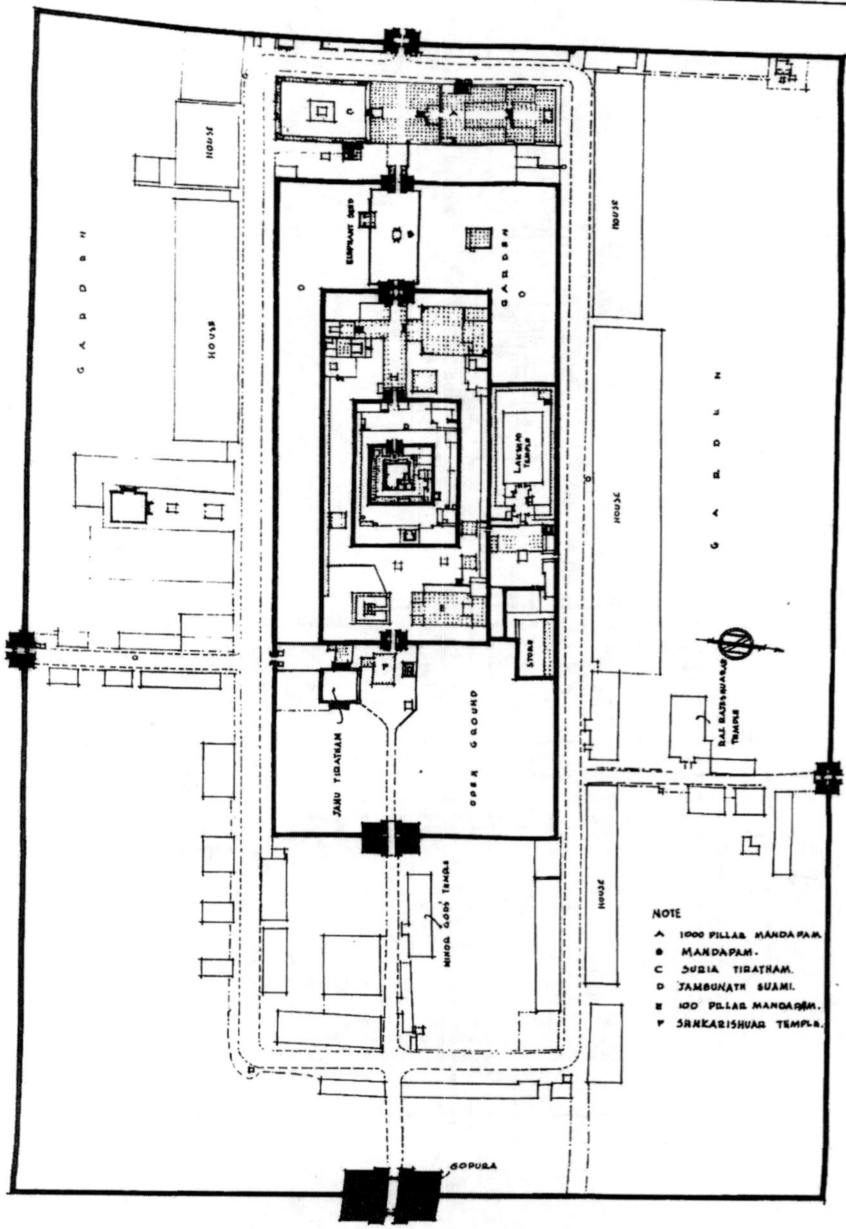

A PLAN OF JAMBUISHUAR TEMPLE, NEAR TRICHINOPOLY, MADRAS

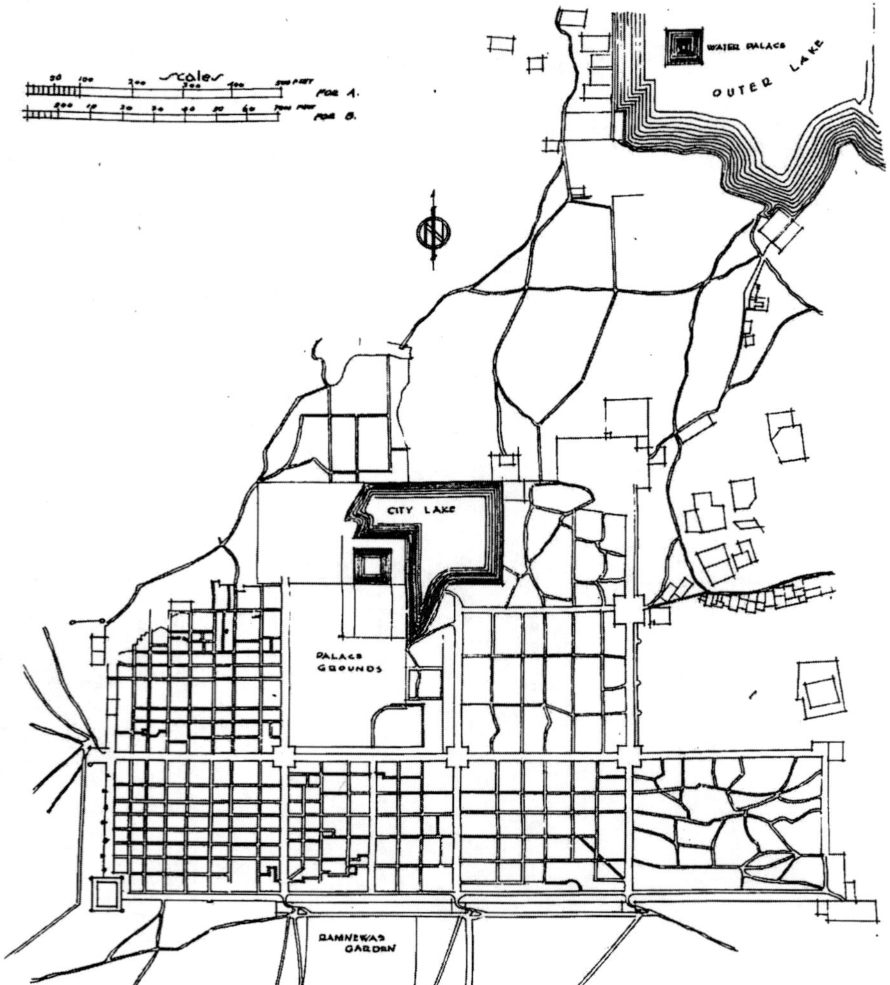

B PLAN OF JAIPUR CITY RAJPUTANA.

MENS. ARCH. SURVEY "TEMPLES IN TRICHINOPOLY"
DELT. L.K. NANDWANA.

PLATE 3

MOHAMEDAN PLANNING

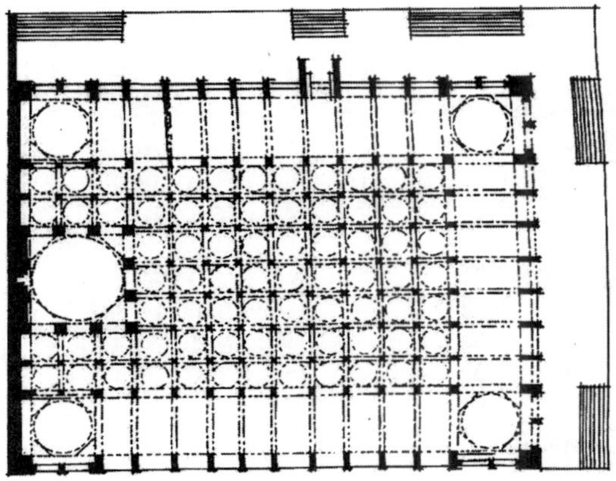

1 MOSQUE AT KULBARGA
1375

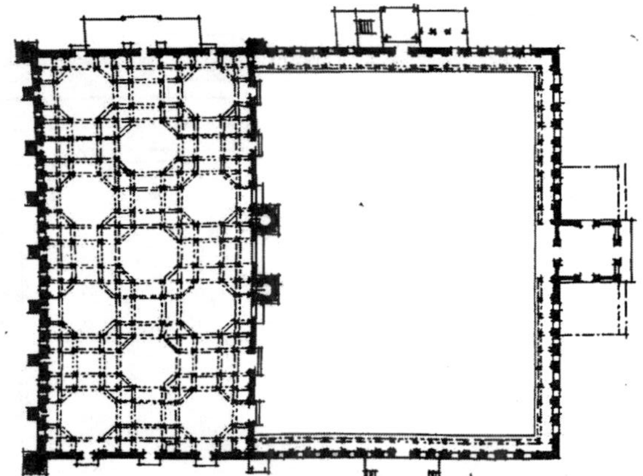

2 JAMI MASJID CHAMPANIR
1500

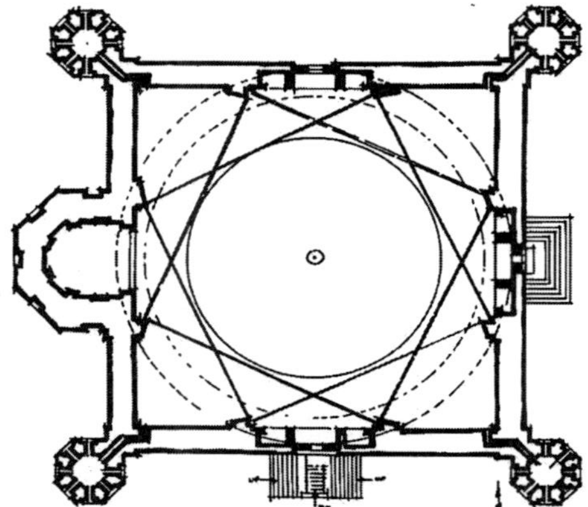

3 GOL GUMBAZ. BIJAPUR.
1625.

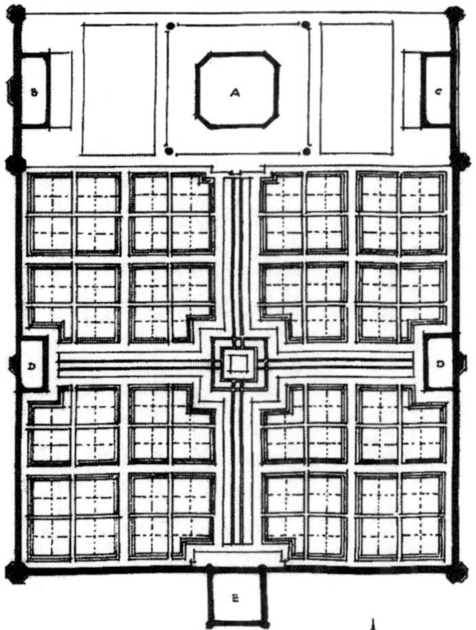

4 TAJ MAHAL AGRA
1630

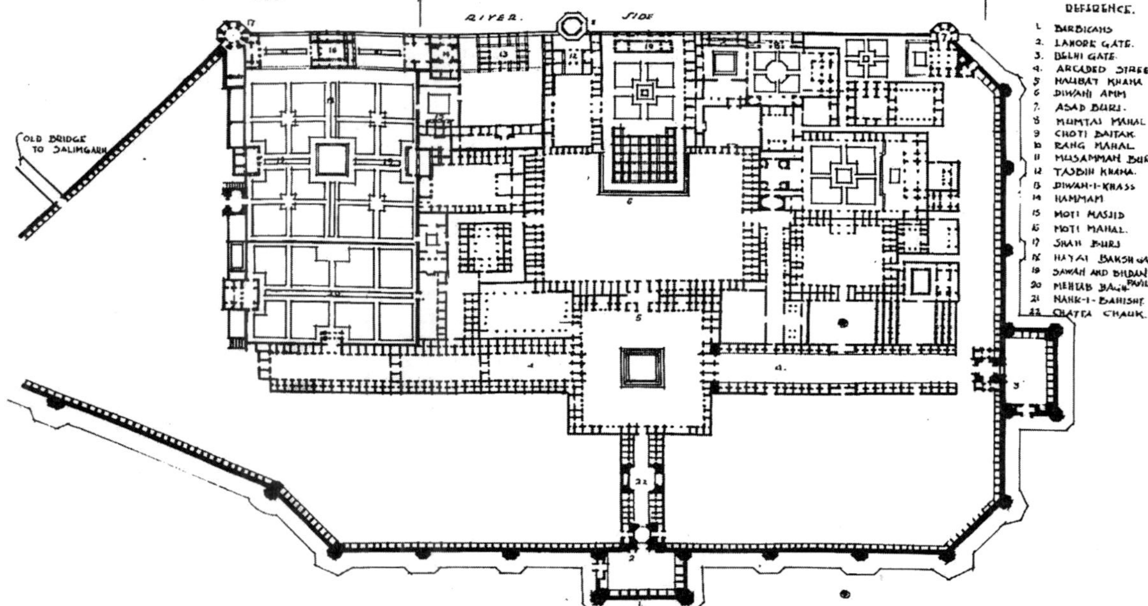

5 PALACE AT DELHI.
1650

DELT. J. VAZ.

BUDDHIST ORDER

KARLI CAVE TEMPLE NEAR POONA.

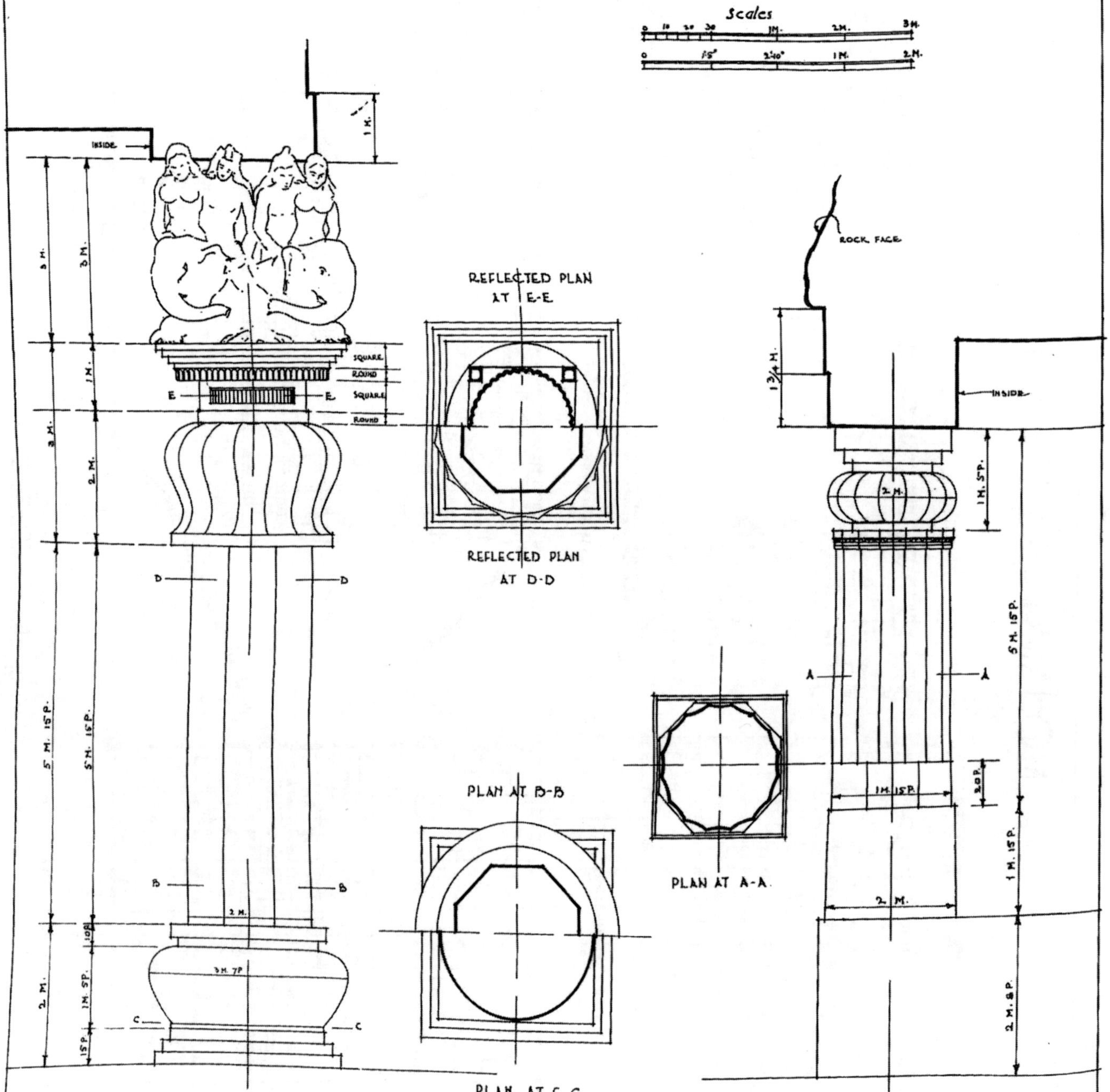

PLAN AT C-C

COLUMN FROM INTERIOR OF KARLI CAVE

COLUMN FROM EXTERIOR OF A ROCK-CUT CAVE ADJACENT TO THE MAIN KARLI CAVE.

MENS V. S. PALSHIKAR.
DELT S. S. PALSHIKAR.

PLATE 5

ANCIENT HINDU ORDER

GENERAL HINDU ORDER (DRAVIDIAN)

ACHUTYA RAYAL'S TEMPLE VIJIANAGAR.

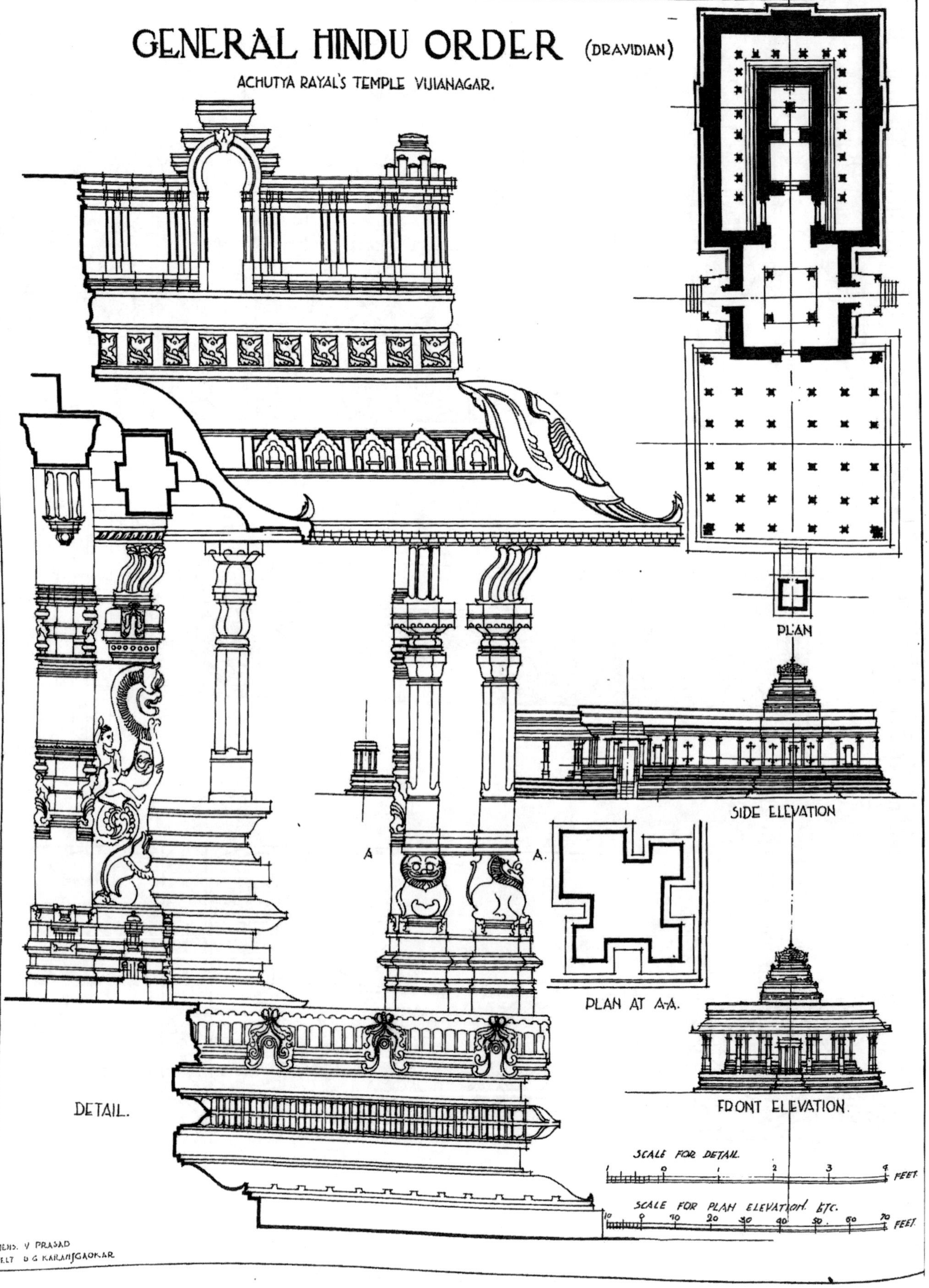

MEAS. V PRASAD
DELT D G KARANJGAOKAR

PLATE 7

GENERAL HINDU ORDER (CHĀLUKYAN)

Ⓐ&Ⓑ PILLARS FROM THE TEMPLE OF ARVATTUKAMBHADA. BANKAPUR.

Ⓒ PILLAR FROM THE TEMPLE OF MADHUKESVARA . BANAVASI.

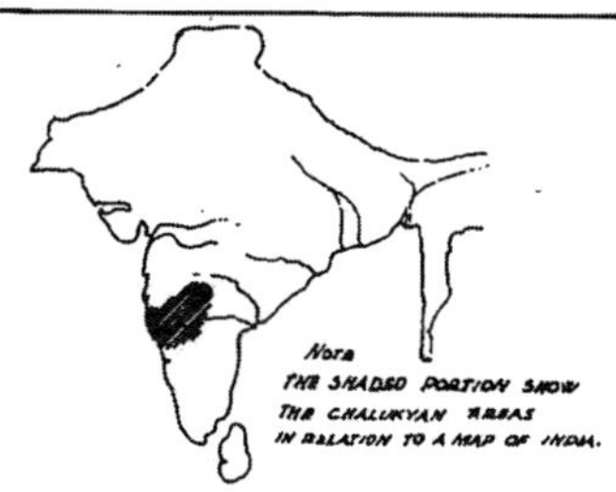

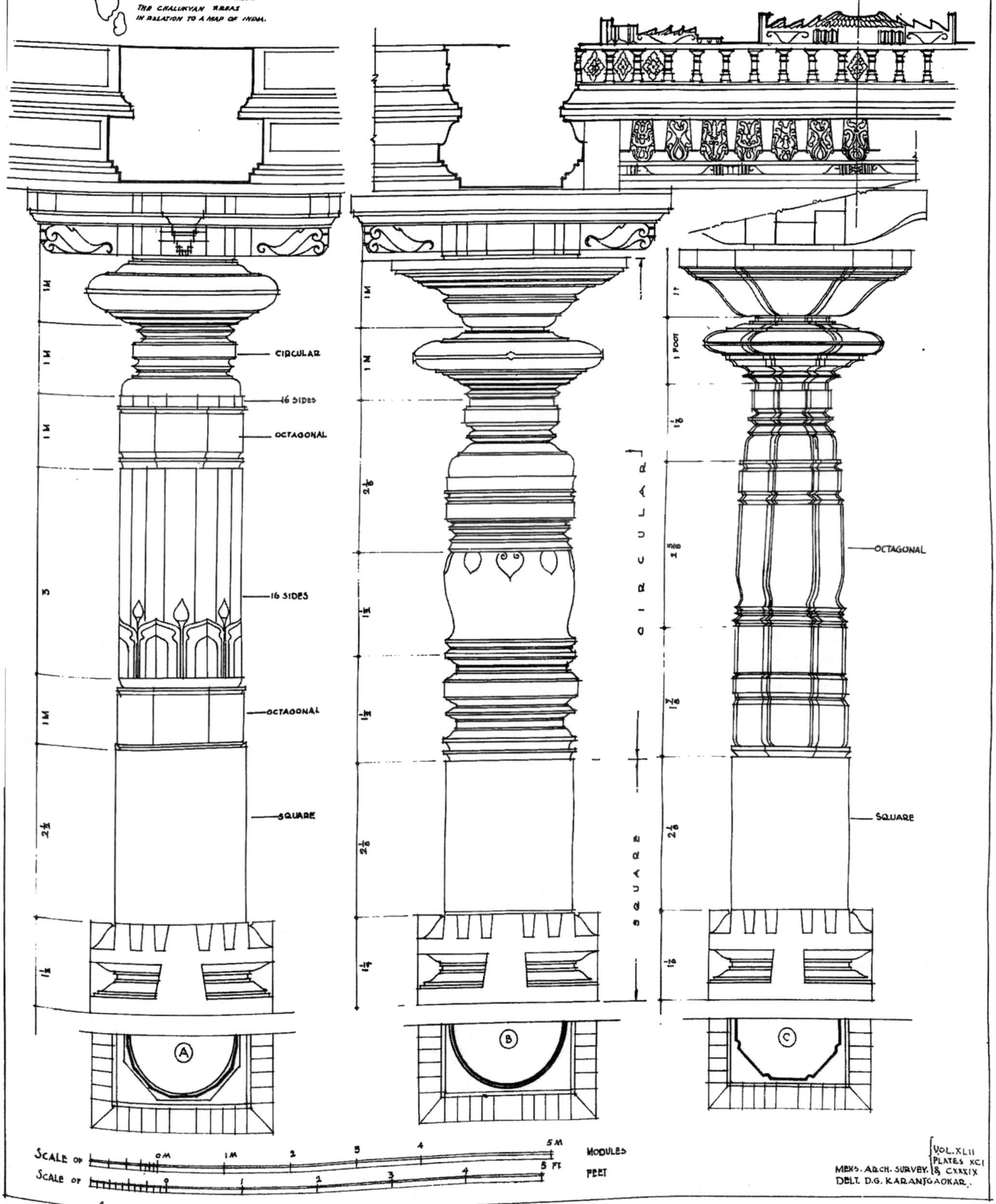

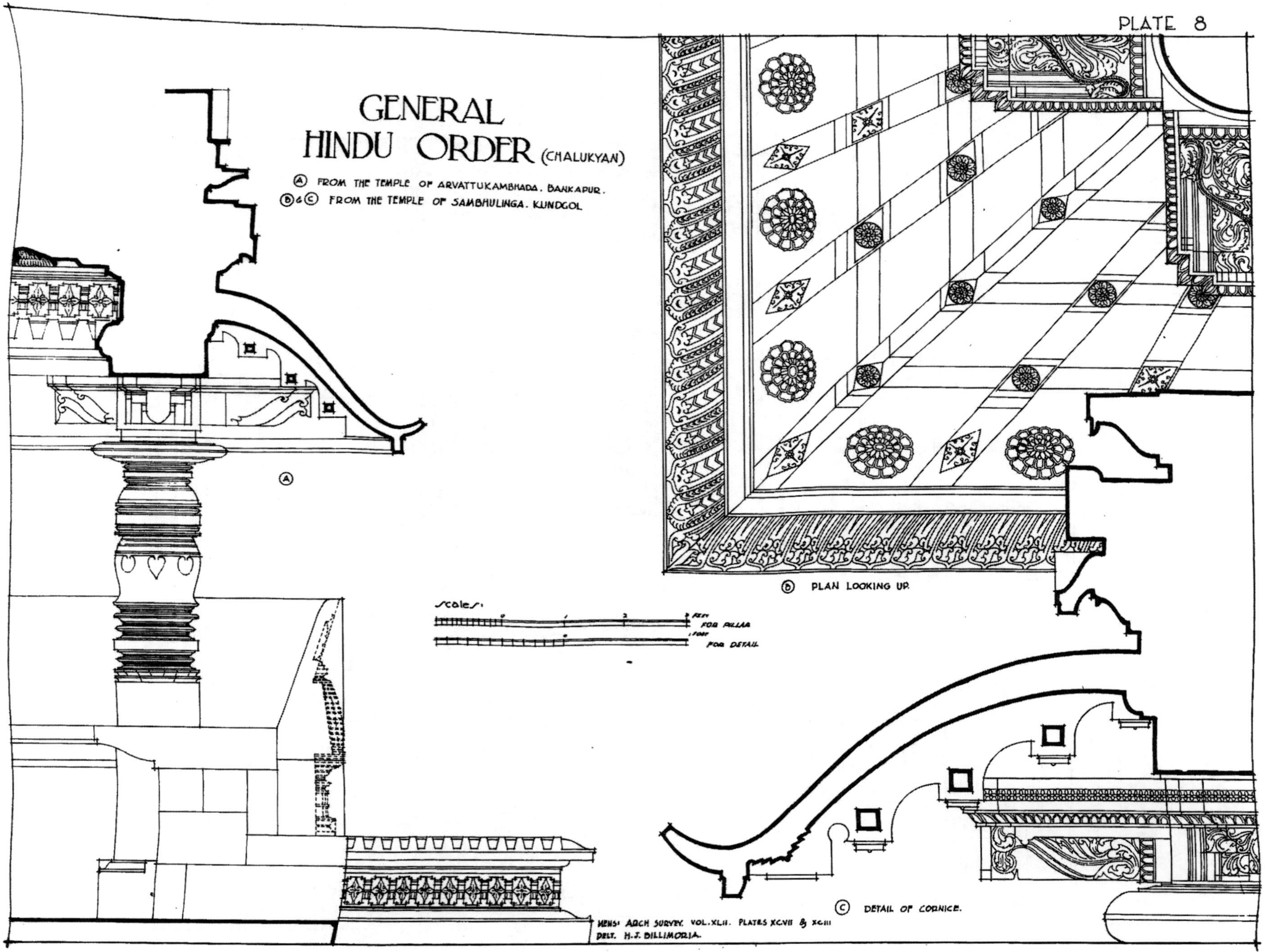
PLATE 8
GENERAL
HINDU ORDER (CHALUKYAN)
Ⓐ FROM THE TEMPLE OF ARVATTUKAMBHADA. BANKAPUR.
Ⓑ & Ⓒ FROM THE TEMPLE OF SAMBHULINGA. KUNDGOL
Ⓐ
Ⓑ PLAN LOOKING UP.
scales:
FOR PILLAR
FOR DETAIL
Ⓒ DETAIL OF CORNICE.
HENS: ARCH SURVEY. VOL. XLII. PLATES XCVII & XCIII
DELT. H. J. BILLIMORIA.

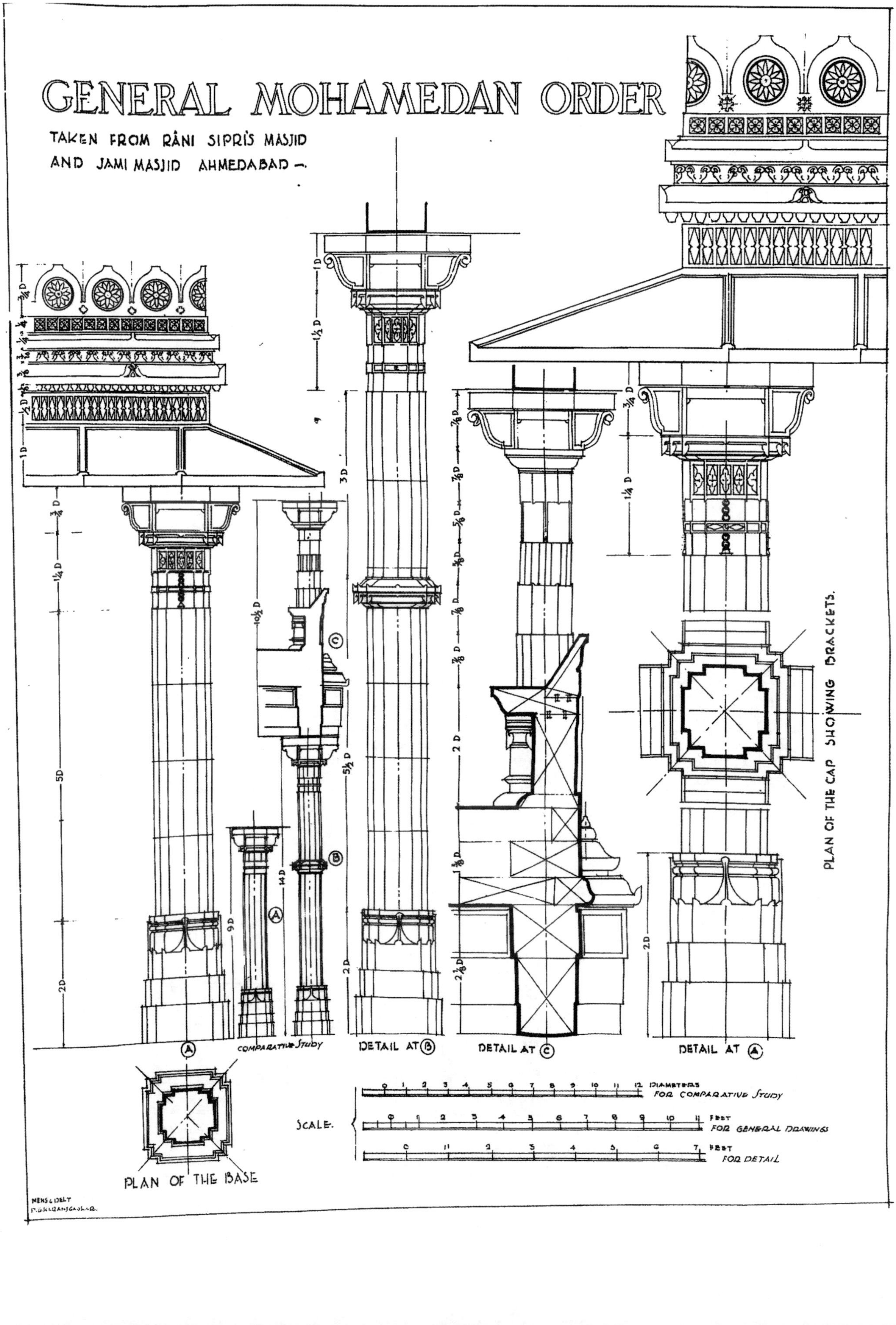
GENERAL MOHAMEDAN ORDER
TAKEN FROM RÂNI SIPRÎS MASJID
AND JAMI MASJID AHMEDABAD —.
COMPARATIVE STUDY
DETAIL AT B
DETAIL AT C
DETAIL AT A
PLAN OF THE CAP SHOWING BRACKETS.
PLAN OF THE BASE
SCALE.
DIAMETERS FOR COMPARATIVE STUDY
FEET FOR GENERAL DRAWINGS
FEET FOR DETAIL

PLATE 10

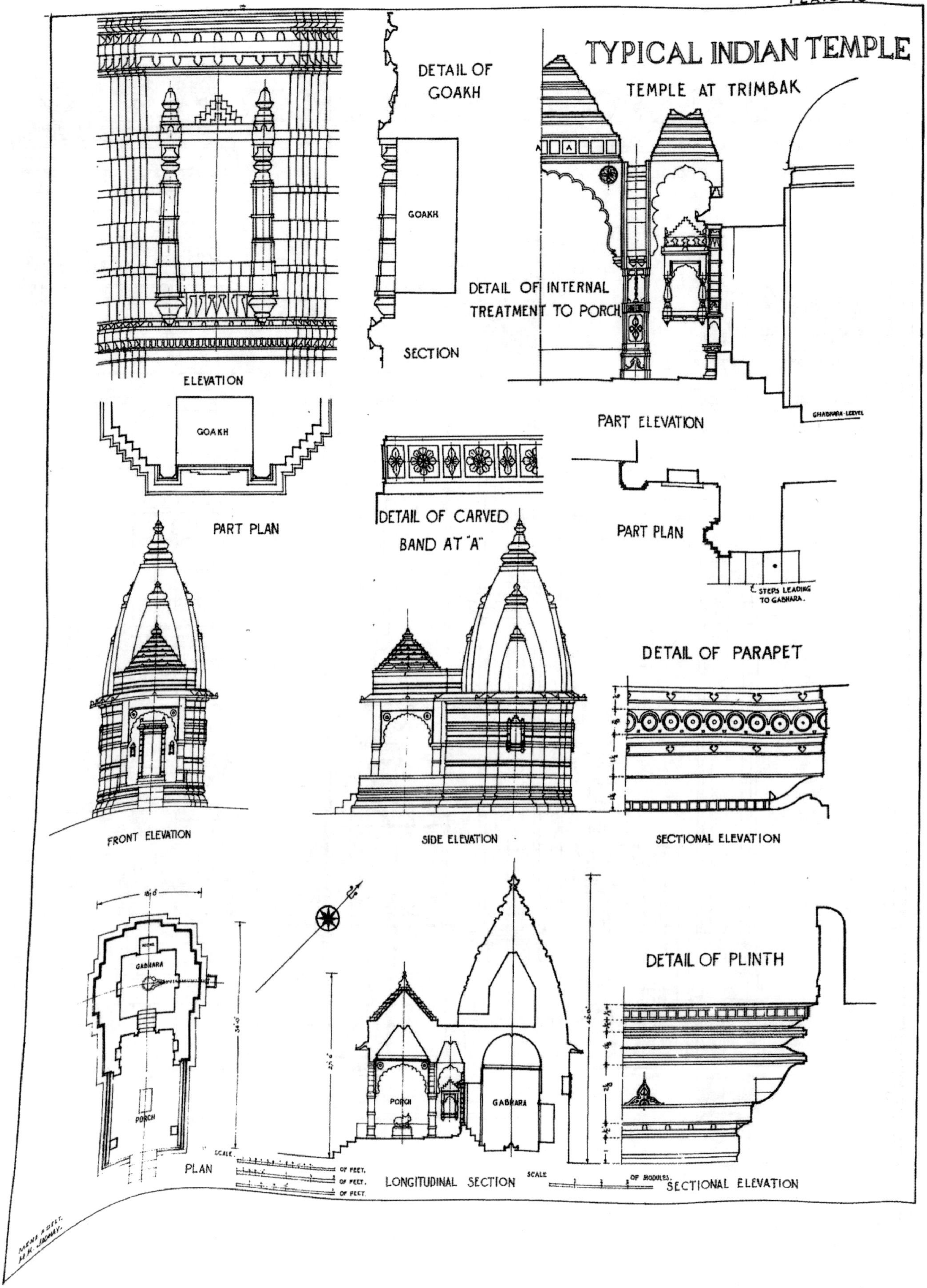
TYPICAL INDIAN TEMPLE
TEMPLE AT TRIMBAK
DETAIL OF GOAKH
GOAKH
SECTION
ELEVATION
DETAIL OF INTERNAL TREATMENT TO PORCH
A
PART ELEVATION
GOAKH
PART PLAN
DETAIL OF CARVED BAND AT "A"
PART PLAN
STEPS LEADING TO GABHARA.
DETAIL OF PARAPET
FRONT ELEVATION
SIDE ELEVATION
SECTIONAL ELEVATION
DETAIL OF PLINTH
NICHE
GABHARA
PORCH
PLAN
SCALE
OF FEET.
OF FEET.
OF FEET.
PORCH
GABHARA
LONGITUDINAL SECTION
SCALE
OF MODULES.
SECTIONAL ELEVATION

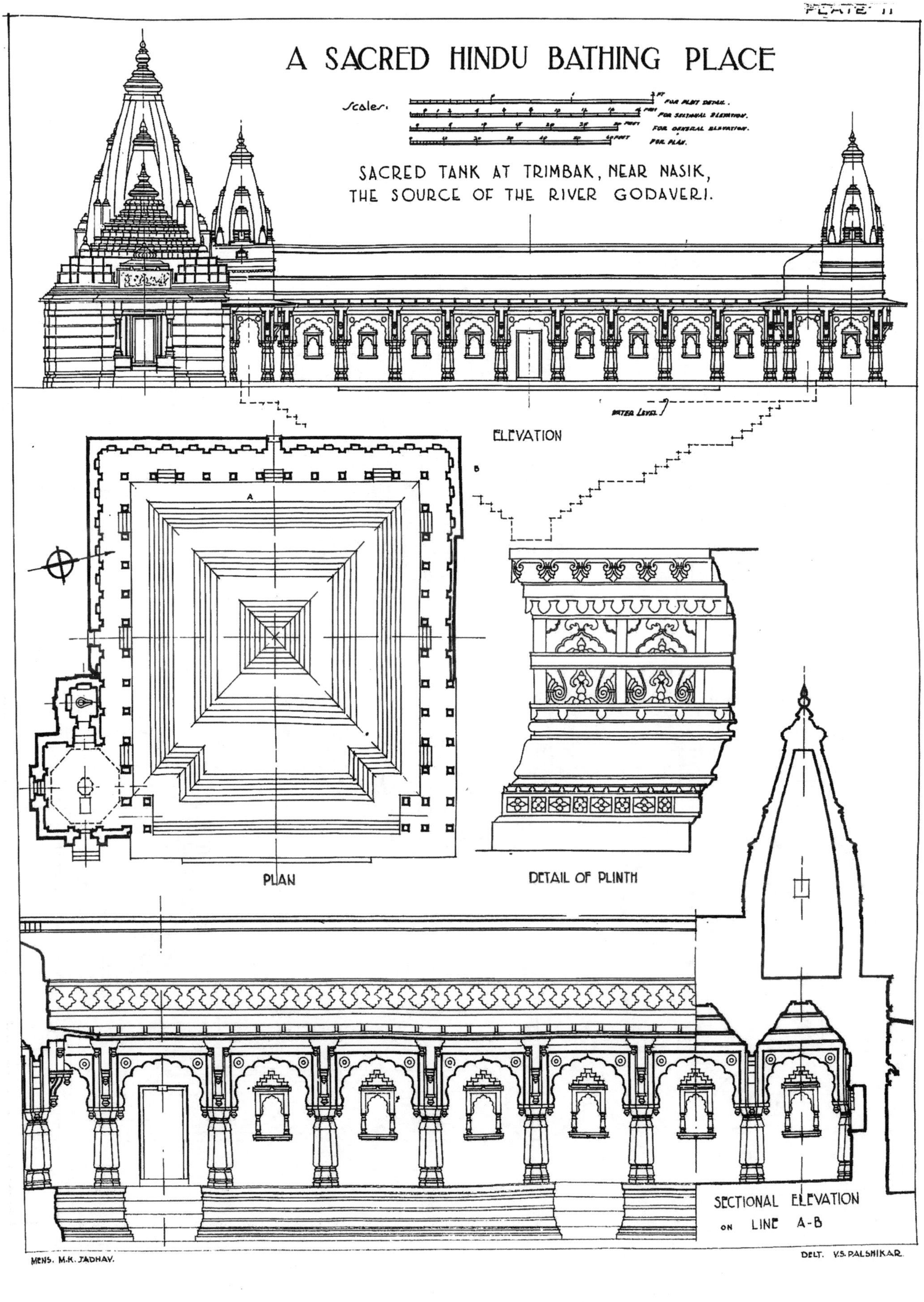

MENS. M.K. JADHAV.

DELT. V.S. PALSHIKAR.

PLATE 12

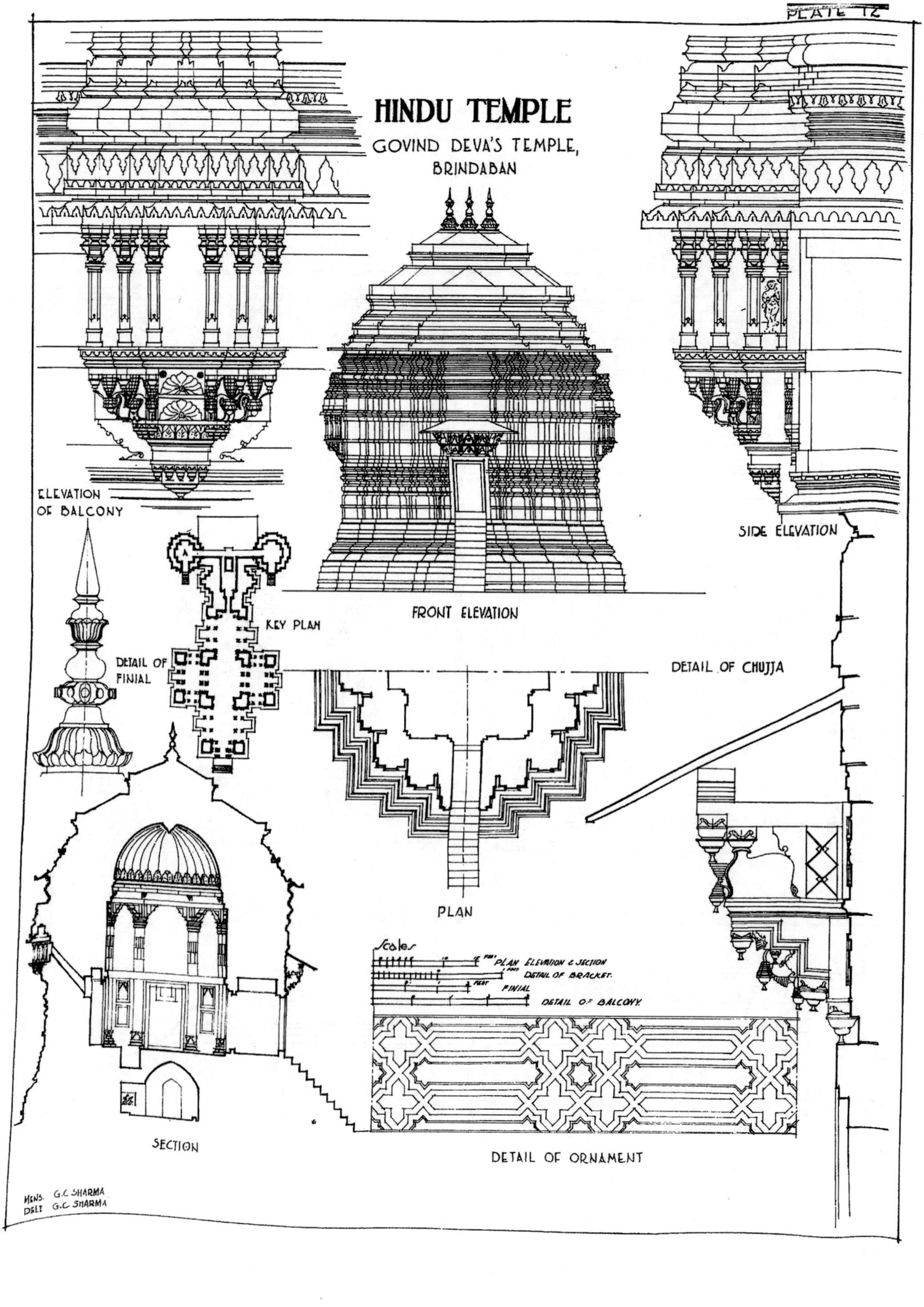
HINDU TEMPLE
GOVIND DEVA'S TEMPLE,
BRINDABAN
ELEVATION OF BALCONY
FRONT ELEVATION
SIDE ELEVATION
KEY PLAN
DETAIL OF FINIAL
DETAIL OF CHUJJA
PLAN
SECTION
Scales
PLAN ELEVATION & SECTION
DETAIL OF BRACKET
FINIAL
DETAIL OF BALCONY
DETAIL OF ORNAMENT
MENS. G.C SHARMA
DELT G.C SHARMA

PLATE 13

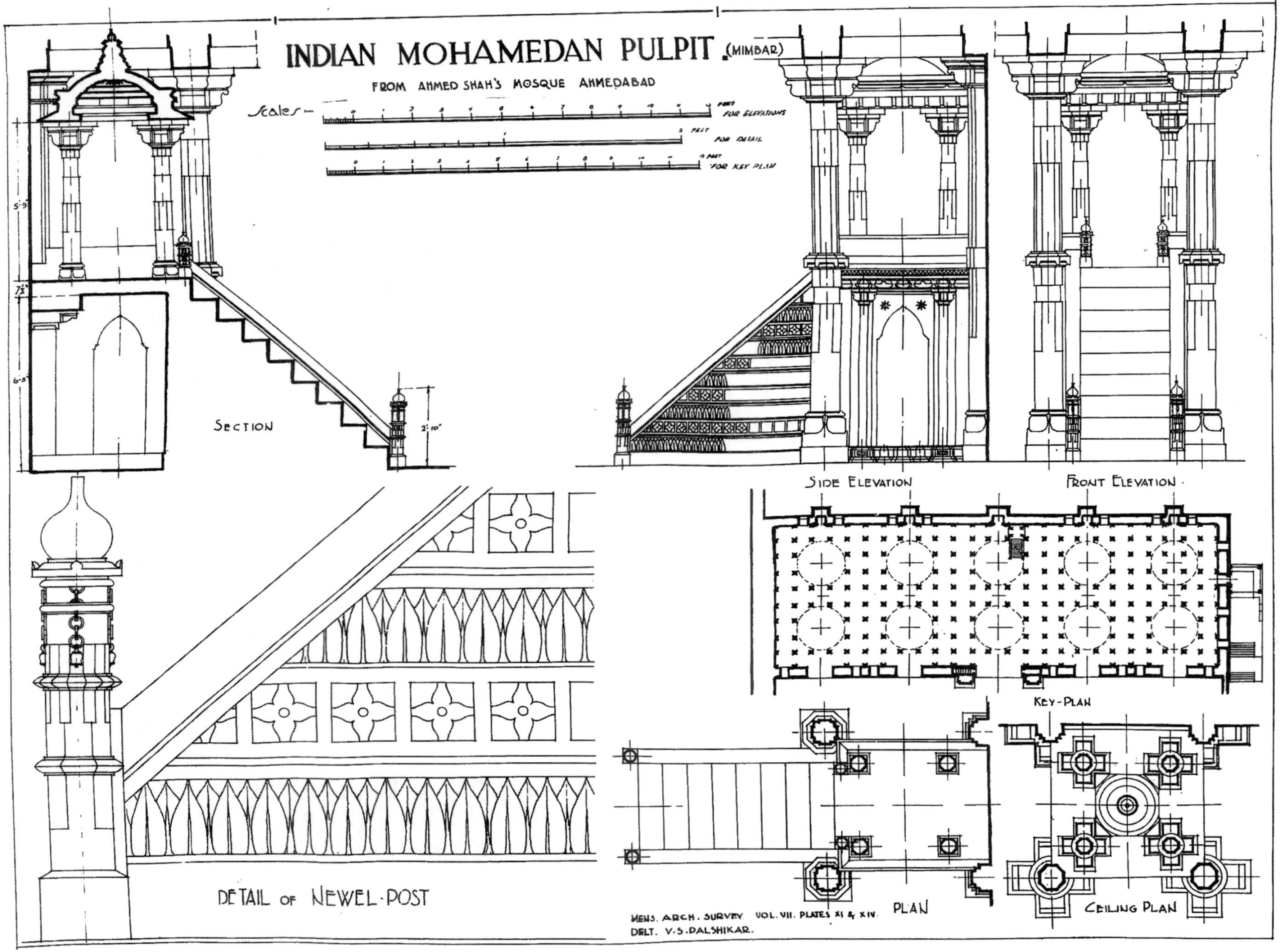
INDIAN MOHAMEDAN PULPIT. (MIMBAR)
FROM AHMED SHAH'S MOSQUE AHMEDABAD
Scales –
FEET FOR ELEVATIONS
FEET FOR DETAIL
FEET FOR KEY PLAN
5'-9"
7½"
6'-5"
2'-10"
SECTION
SIDE ELEVATION
FRONT ELEVATION
KEY-PLAN
DETAIL OF NEWEL-POST
PLAN
CEILING PLAN
MEMS. ARCH. SURVEY VOL. VII. PLATES XI & XIV.
DELT. V. S. DALSHIKAR.

PLATE 14

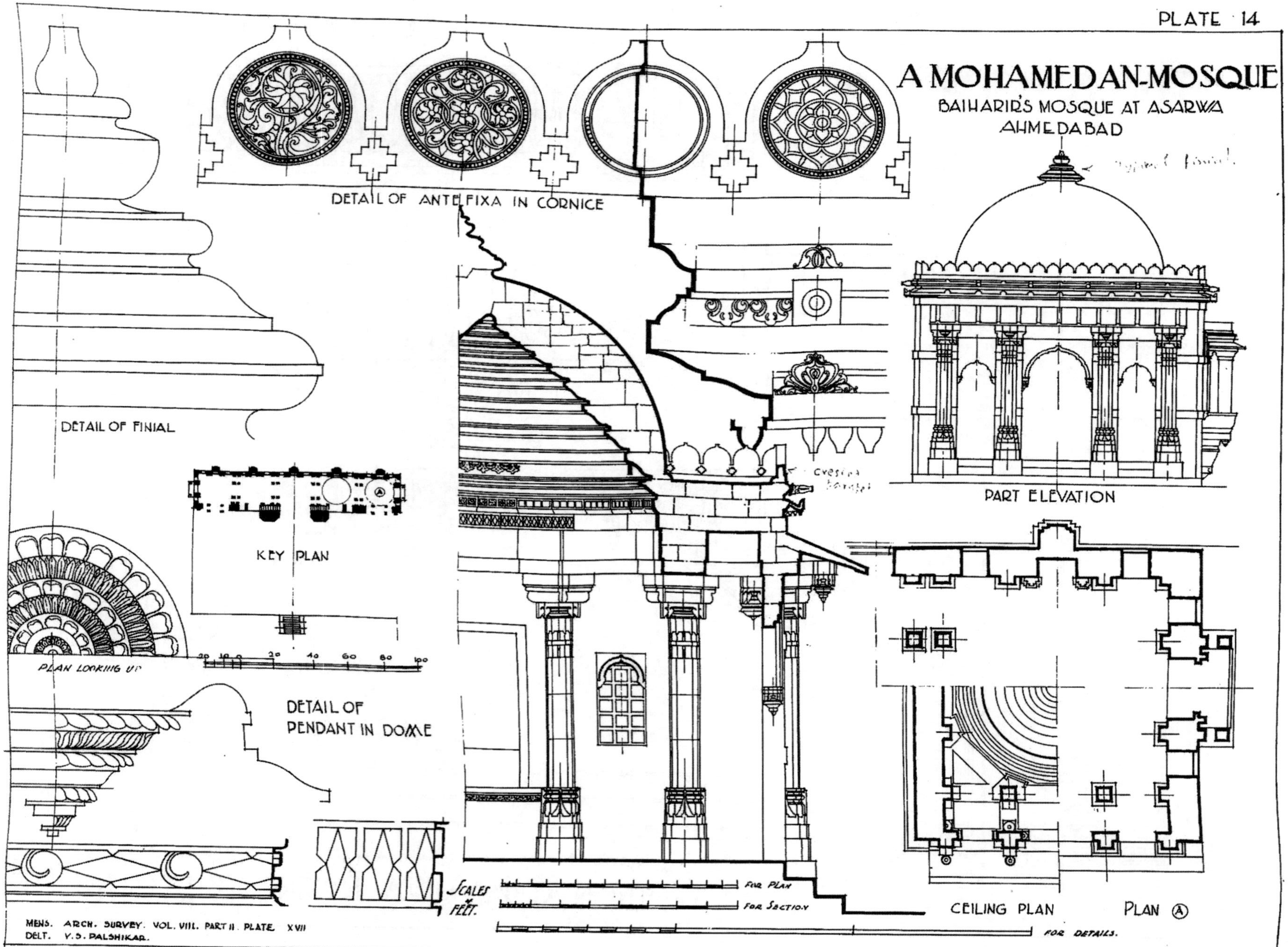
A MOHAMEDAN-MOSQUE
BAIHARIR'S MOSQUE AT ASARWA
AHMEDABAD
DETAIL OF ANTEFIXA IN CORNICE
DETAIL OF FINIAL
KEY PLAN
PLAN LOOKING UP
DETAIL OF PENDANT IN DOME
PART ELEVATION
CEILING PLAN
PLAN Ⓐ
SCALES OF FEET.
FOR PLAN
FOR SECTION
FOR DETAILS.
20 10 0 20 40 60 80 100
MENS. ARCH. SURVEY. VOL. VIII. PART II. PLATE XVII
DELT. V. S. PALSHIKAR.

A MOHAMEDAN CHATRI

ENTRANCE PAVILION TO BAI-HARIR'S WELL AT ASARWA.
AHMEDABAD.

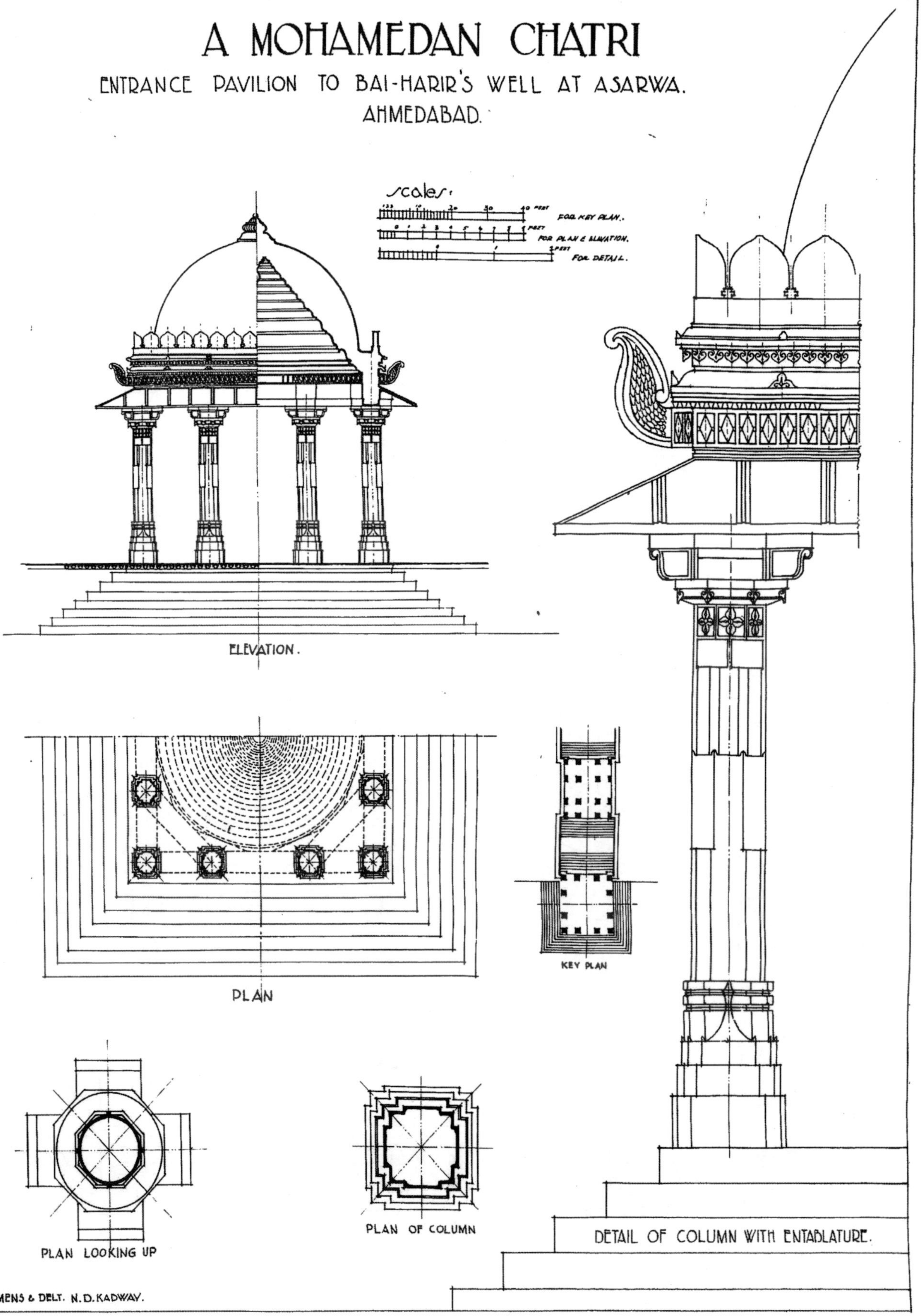

MENS & DELT. N. D. KADWAY.

MOHAMEDAN ENRICHED MOULDINGS

FROM BAI-HARIR'S TOMB, AHMEDABAD.

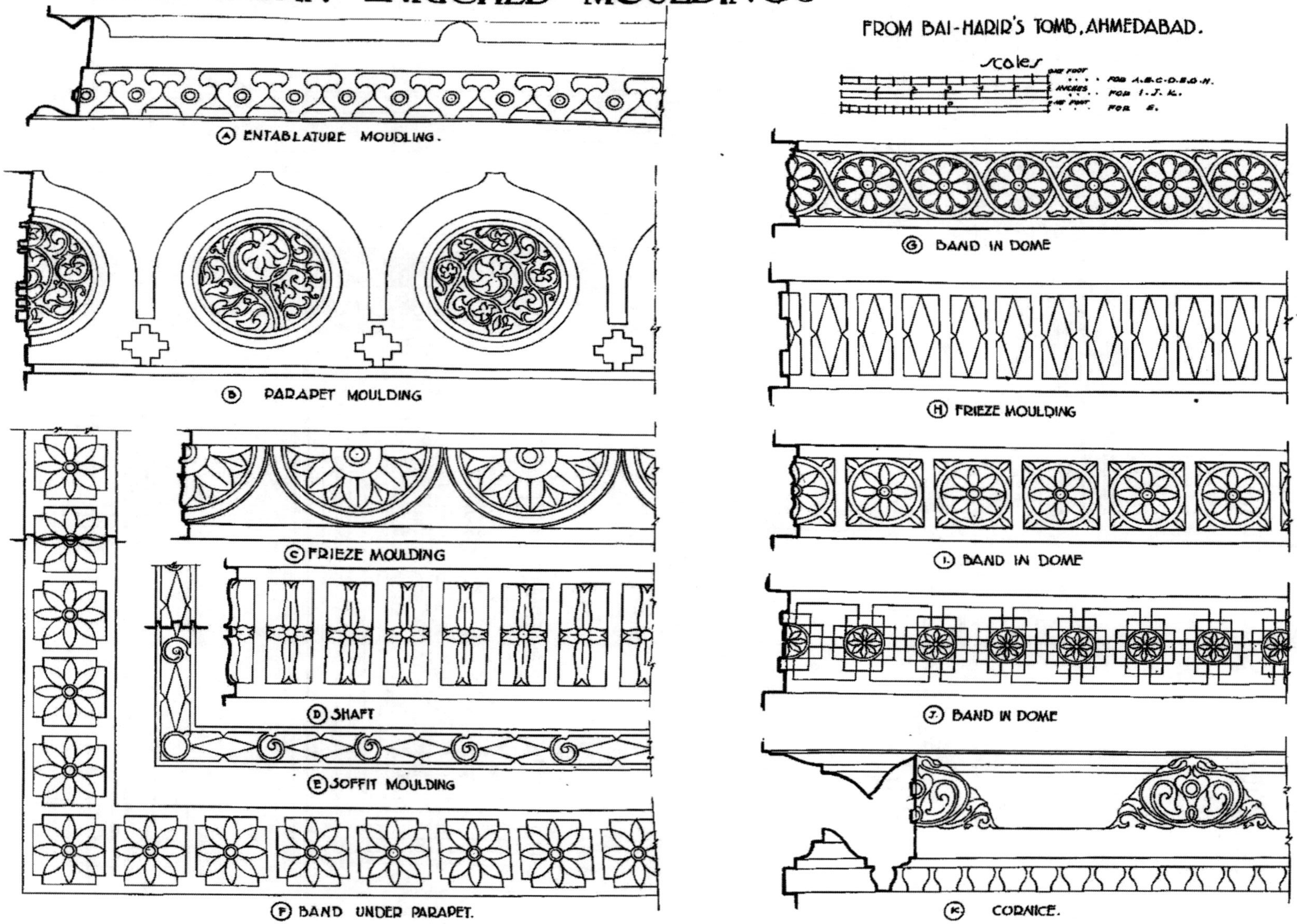

MENS: N.N. DALLAS
DELT: K.P. BURJO-BEHRAM.

A MOHAMEDAN MIHRAB

FROM RANI SIPRI'S MOSQUE, AHMEDABAD

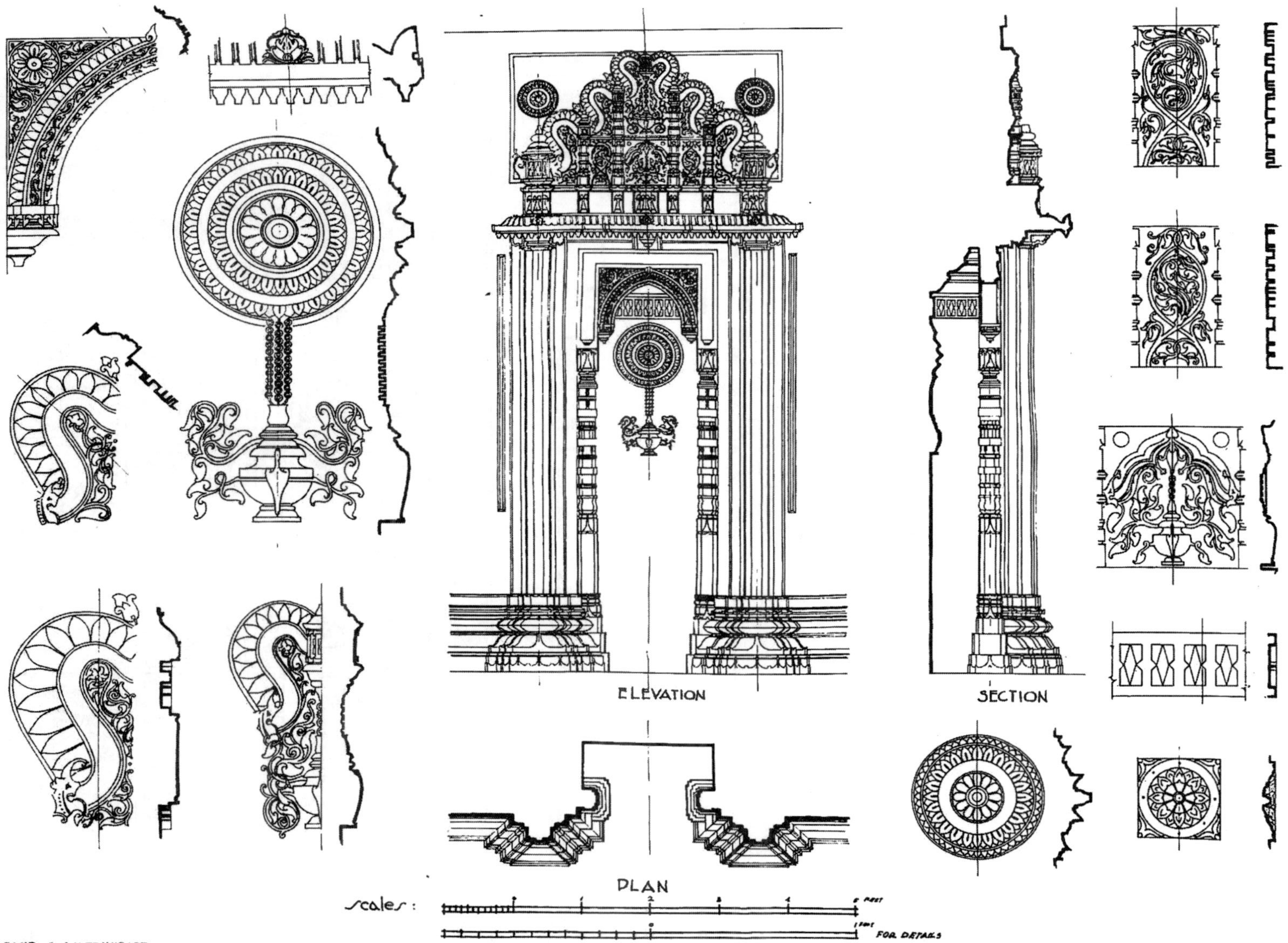

MENS. A.C.VAZ. & A.X.TRINIDADE.
DELT. S.B. UMRIGAR.

PLATE 18

A MOHAMEDAN WINDOW
FROM THE DAYA HALIMA'S TOMB, AHMEDABAD.
ELEVATION OF REAR WINDOW.
SECTION
scales
1 FOOT
FOR PLAN ELEVATION & SECTION
INCHES
FOR DETAIL.
DETAIL OF ORNAMENT BELOW WINDOW.
MENS. R.A SHIRODKAR.
DELT. S.A.MANTRI.

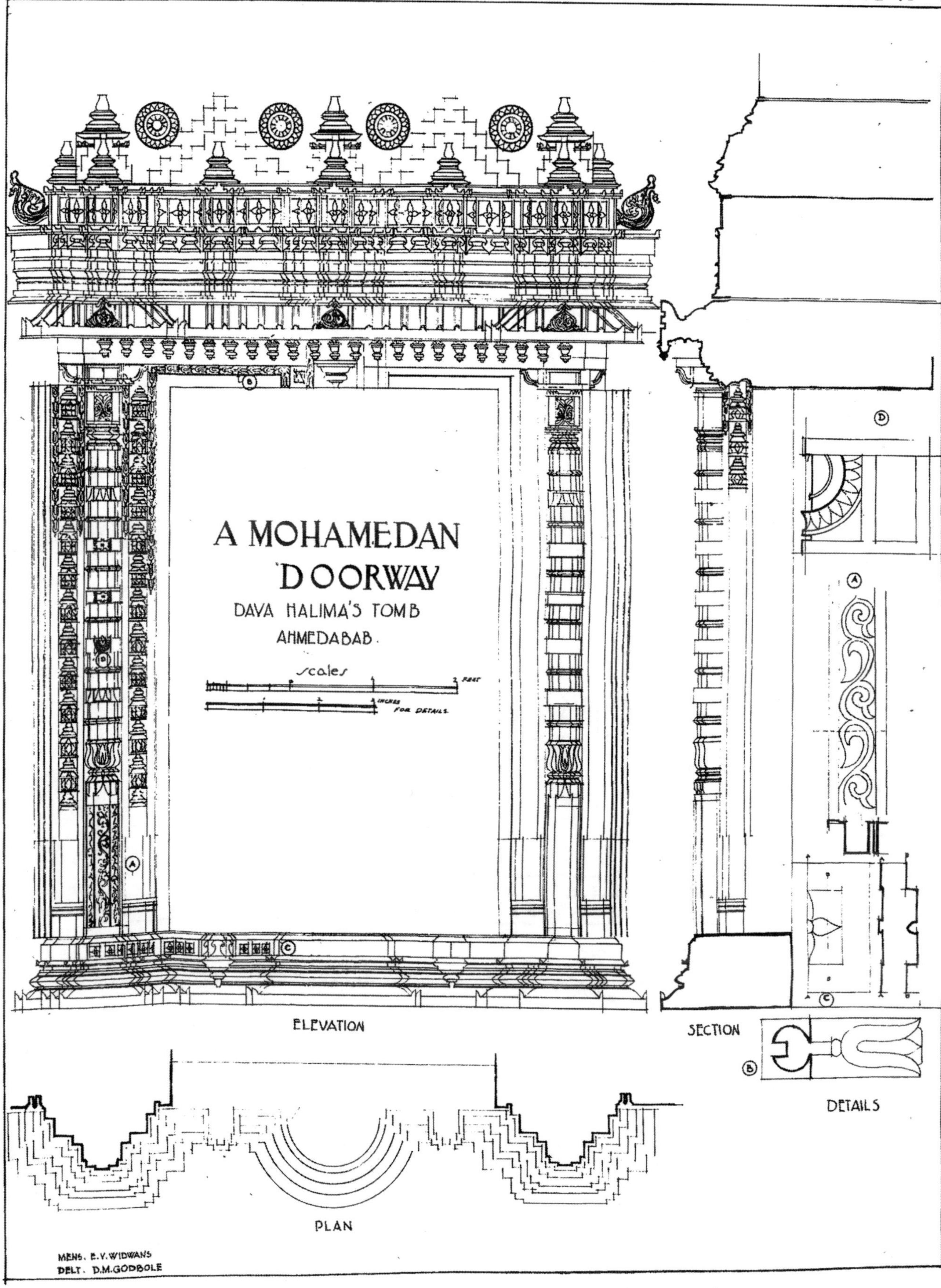
A MOHAMEDAN DOORWAY
DAVA HALIMA'S TOMB
AHMEDABAB.
scales
FEET
INCHES FOR DETAILS.
ELEVATION
SECTION
DETAILS
PLAN
MENS. E.V.WIDWANS
DELT. D.M.GODBOLE

MOHAMEDAN JALIS

FROM AHMEDABAD

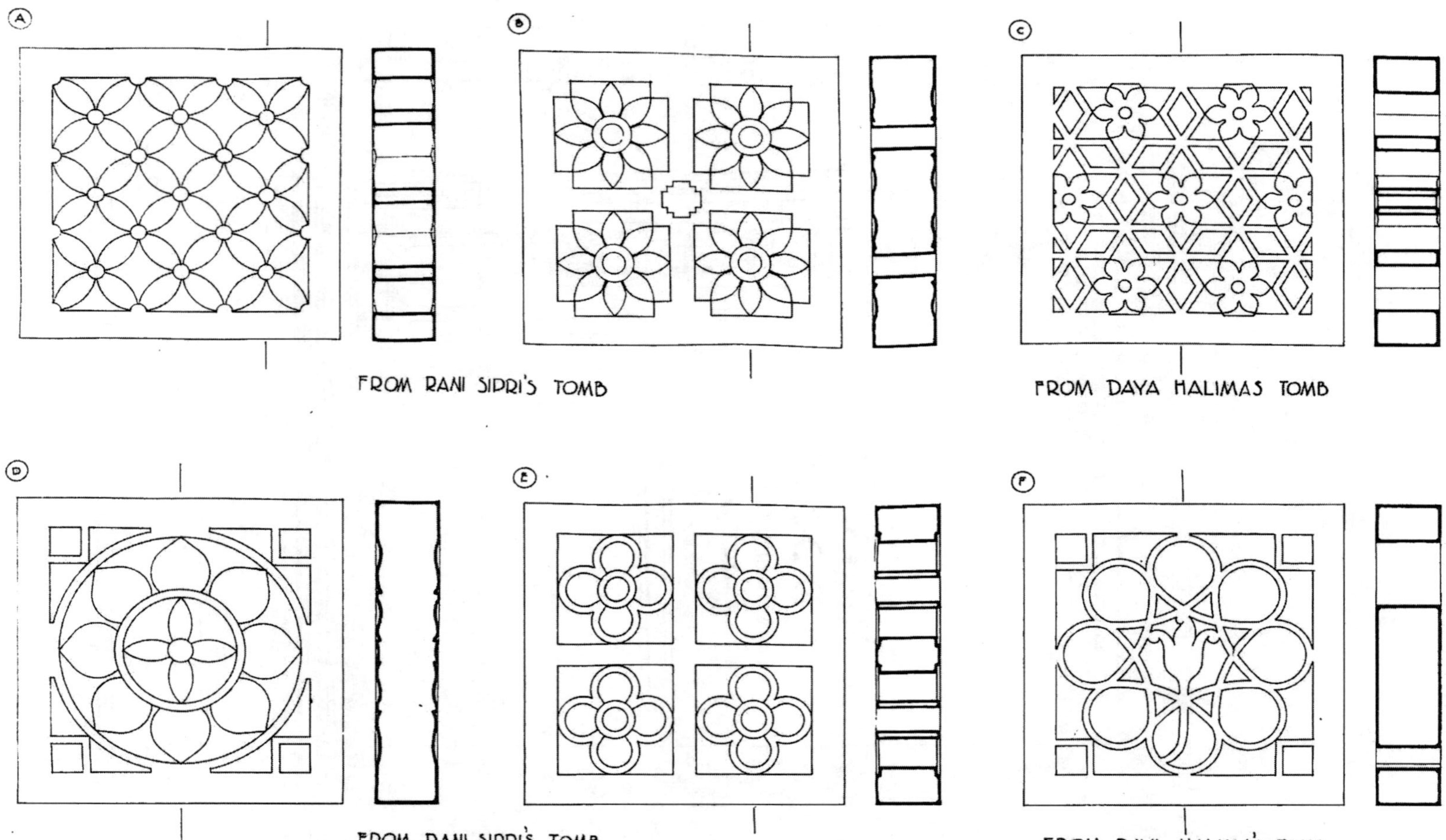

FROM RANI SIPRI'S TOMB (A, B, D, E)

FROM DAYA HALIMA'S TOMB (C, F)

Scale — INCHES FOR A.B.D.E — INCHES FOR C & F.

MENS: R.A. SHIRODKAR, H.B. MORENA, S.A. PENDHARKAR
DELT. S.B. UMRIGAR

PLATE 21

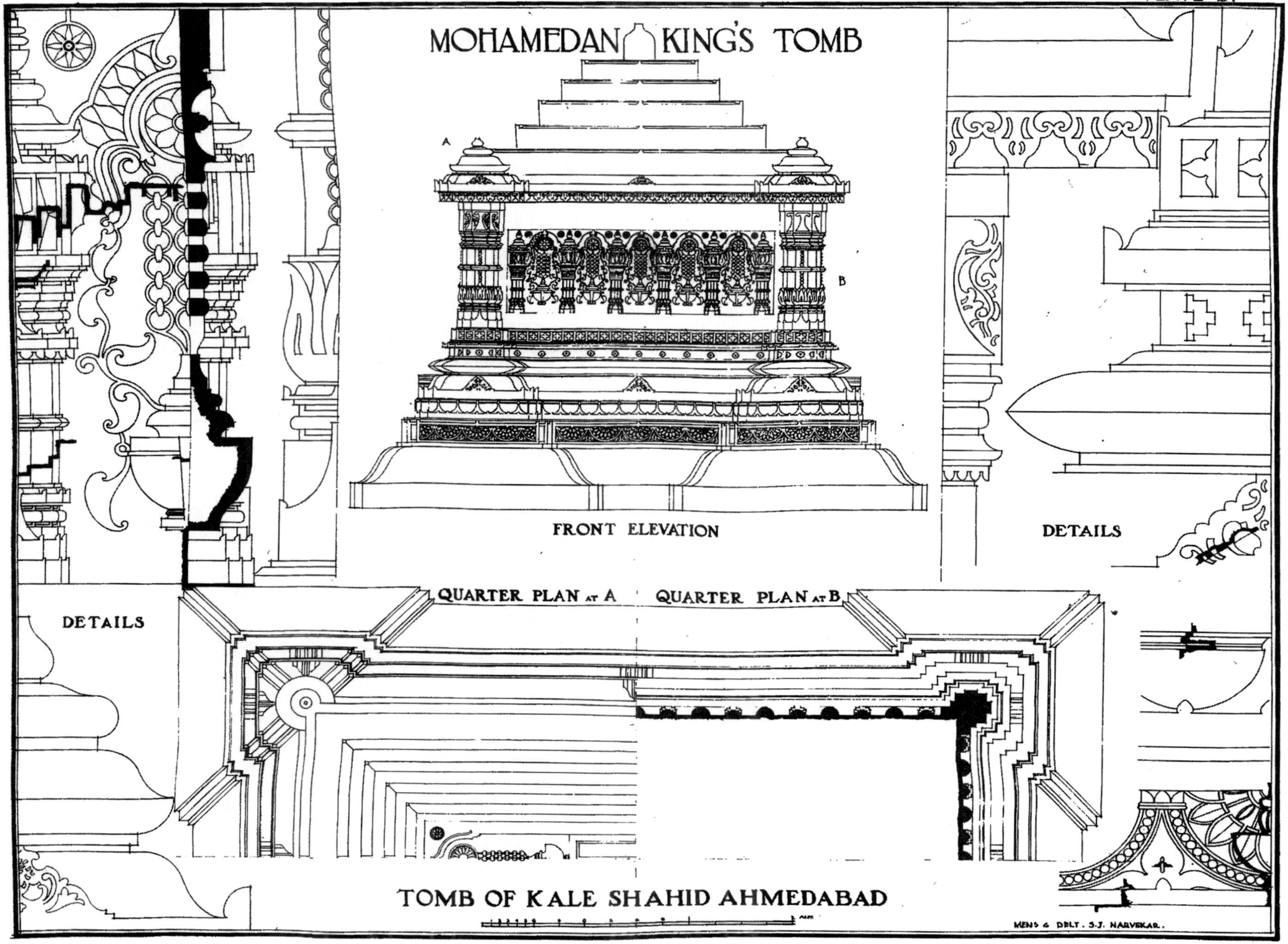
MOHAMEDAN KING'S TOMB
A
B
FRONT ELEVATION
DETAILS
DETAILS
QUARTER PLAN AT A
QUARTER PLAN AT B
TOMB OF KALE SHAHID AHMEDABAD
MENS & DELT. S.J. NARVEKAR.

PLATE 22

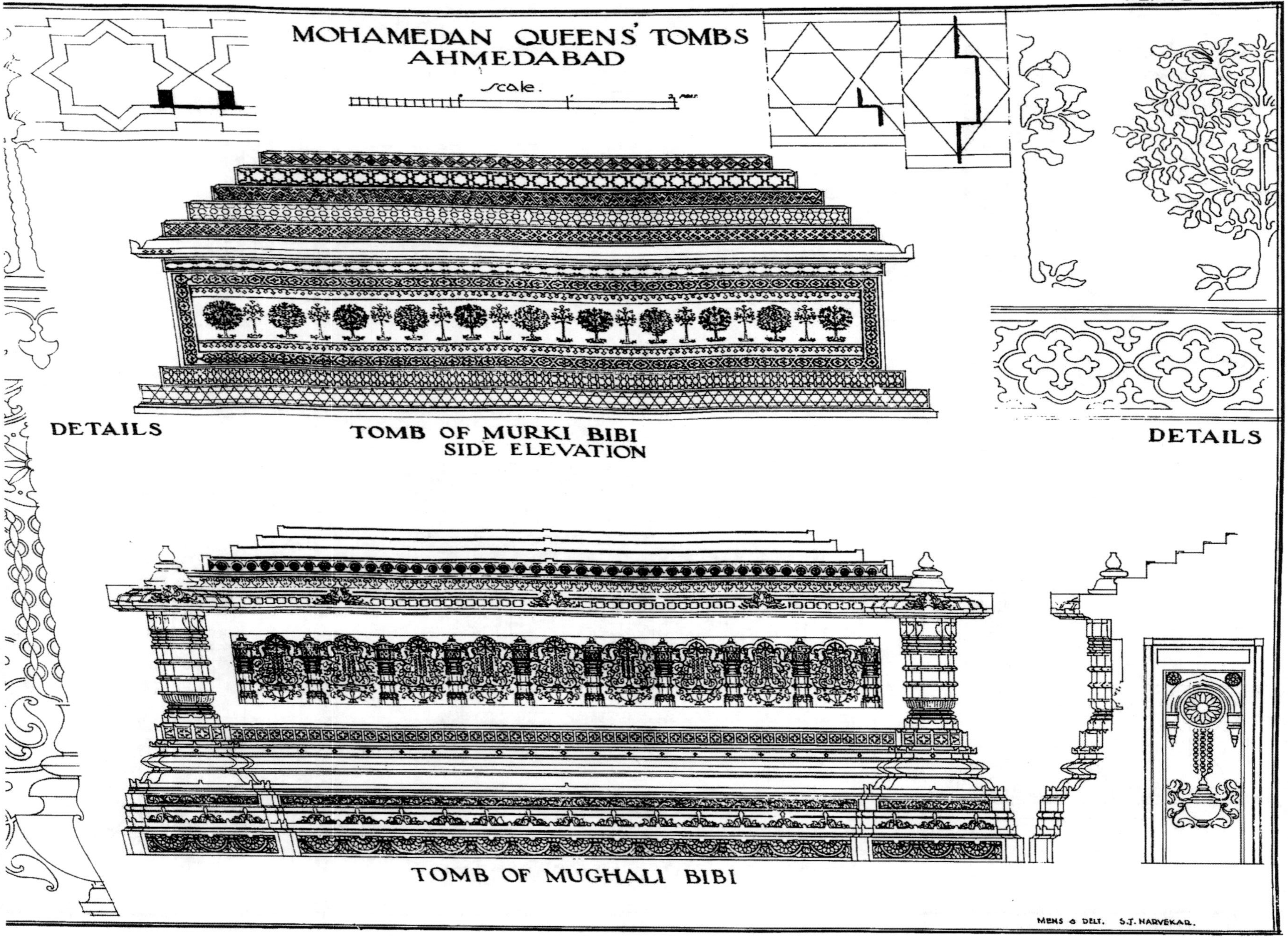
MOHAMEDAN QUEENS' TOMBS
AHMEDABAD
scale.
DETAILS
TOMB OF MURKI BIBI
SIDE ELEVATION
DETAILS
TOMB OF MUGHALI BIBI
MENS & DELT. S.J. NARVEKAR.

A MOHAMEDAN COLONNADE

TWO-STOREYED COLONNADE OVERLOOKING GREAT TANK AT SARKHEJ.

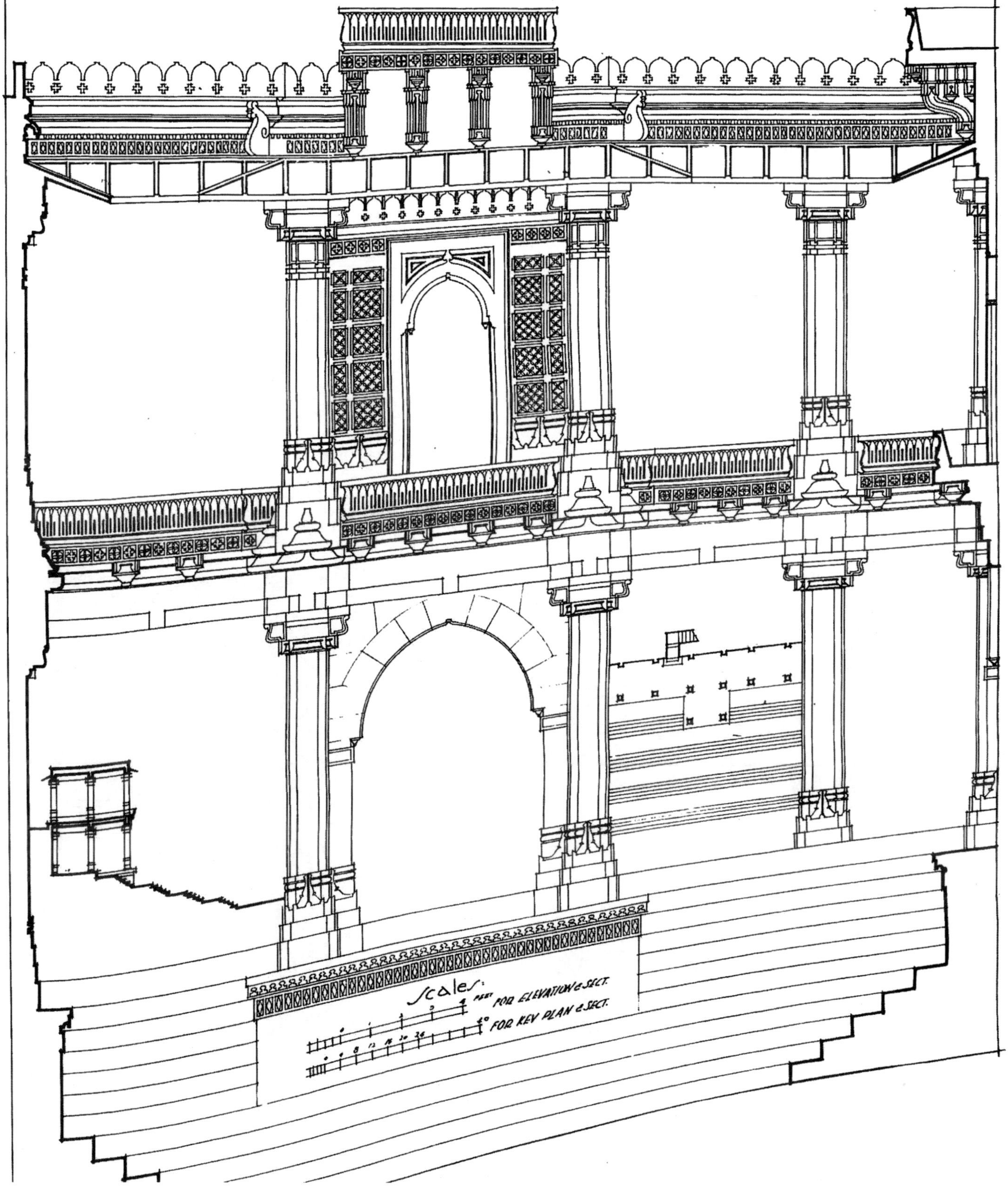

PLATE 24

MOHAMEDAN SLUICES

FROM ANHILWADA PATAN AND KANKARIYA, AHMEDABAD.

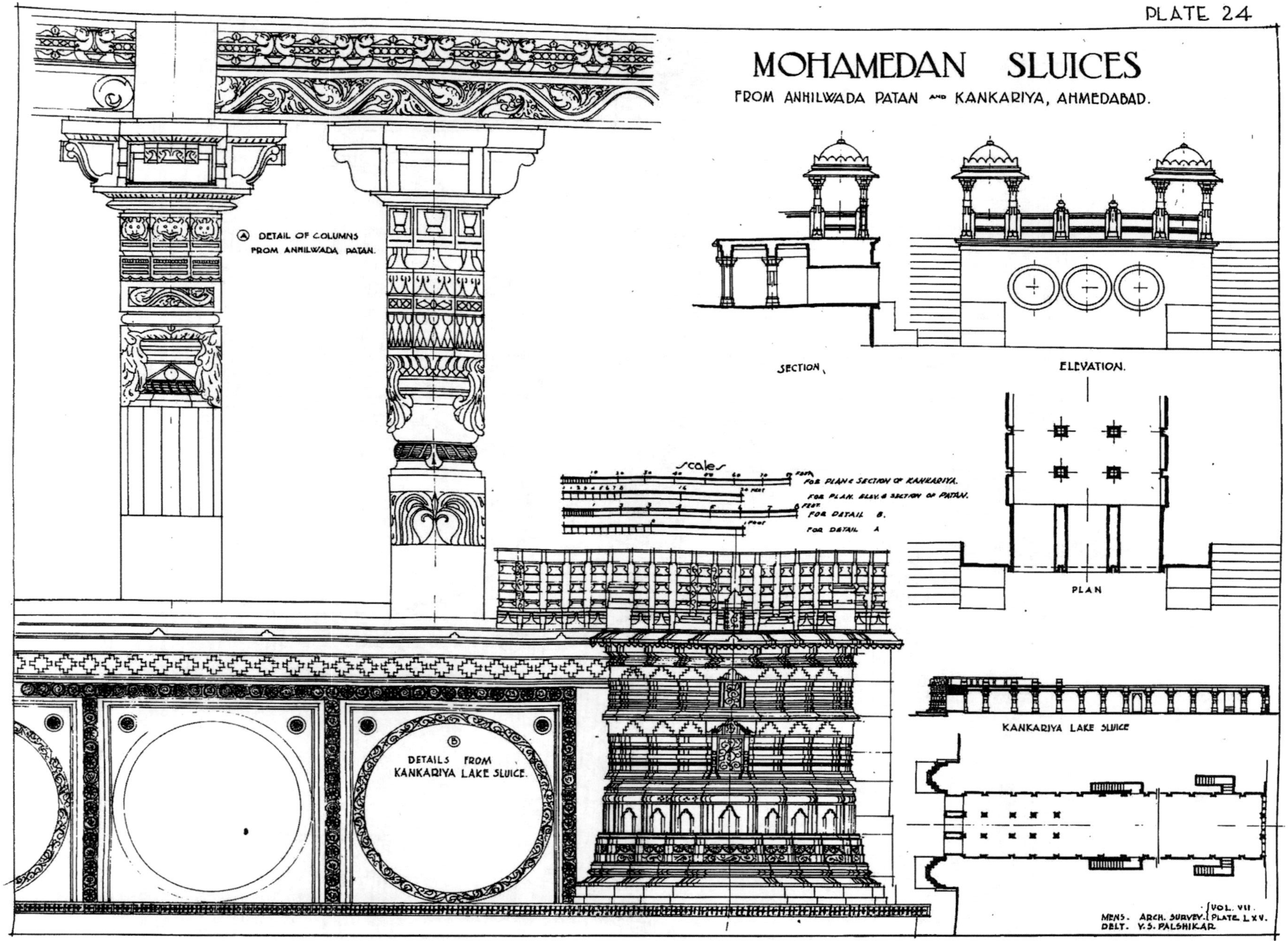

MENS. ARCH. SURVEY. { VOL. VII. PLATE LXV.
DELT. V.S. PALSHIKAR

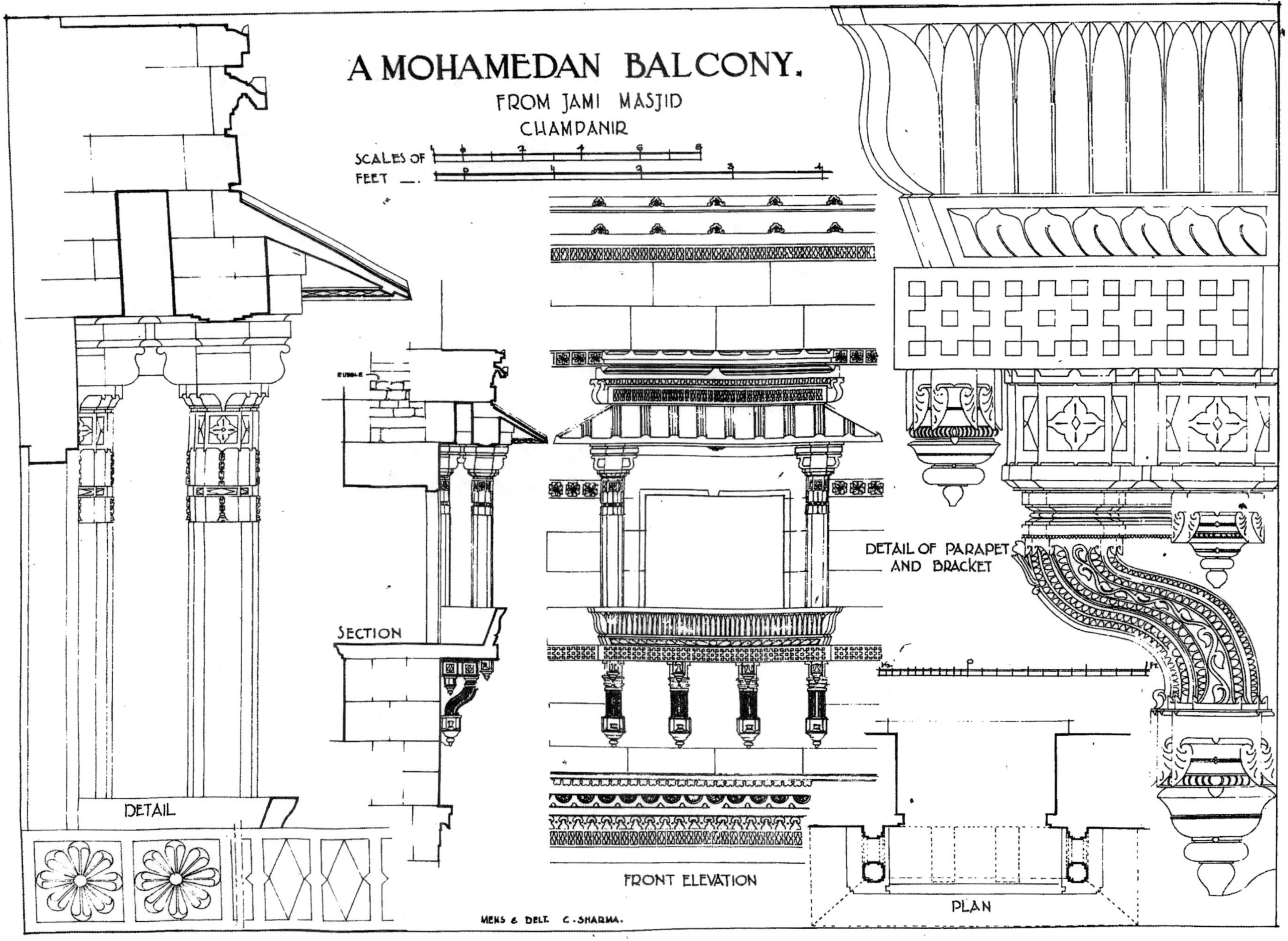
A MOHAMEDAN BALCONY.
FROM JAMI MASJID
CHAMPANIR
SCALES OF
FEET
RUBBLE
DETAIL
SECTION
FRONT ELEVATION
DETAIL OF PARAPET
AND BRACKET
PLAN
MENS & DELT. C. SHARMA.

PLATE 26

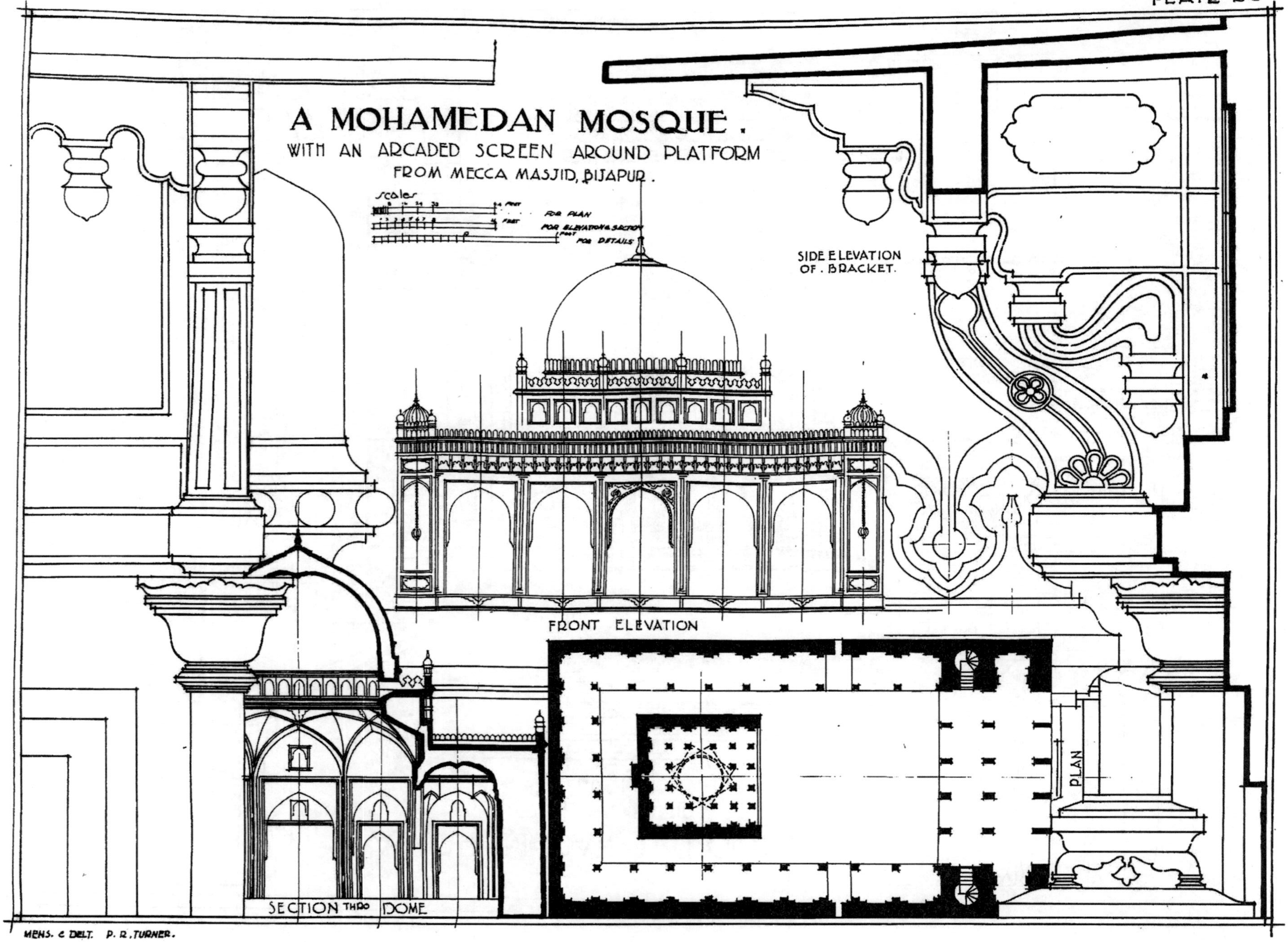
A MOHAMEDAN MOSQUE.
WITH AN ARCADED SCREEN AROUND PLATFORM
FROM MECCA MASJID, BIJAPUR.
scales
FOR PLAN
FOR ELEVATION & SECTION
FOR DETAILS
SIDE ELEVATION OF. BRACKET.
FRONT ELEVATION
PLAN
SECTION THRO DOME
MENS. & DELT. P. R. TURNER.

A MOHAMEDAN MOSQUE

MALIKA JAHAN'S MOSQUE AT BIJAPUR

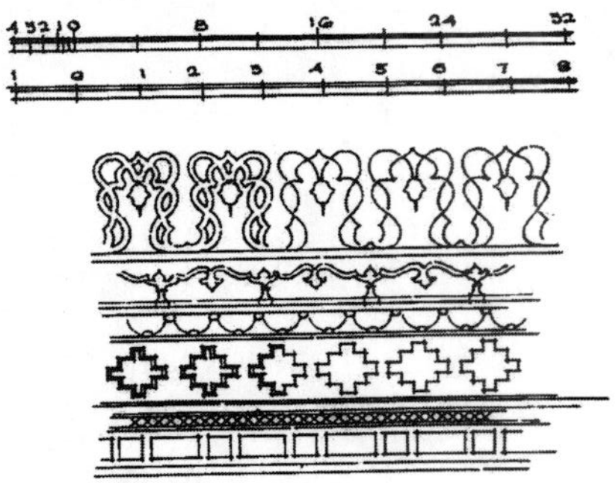

HALF · INCH DETAIL OF PARAPET.

FRONT ELEVATION

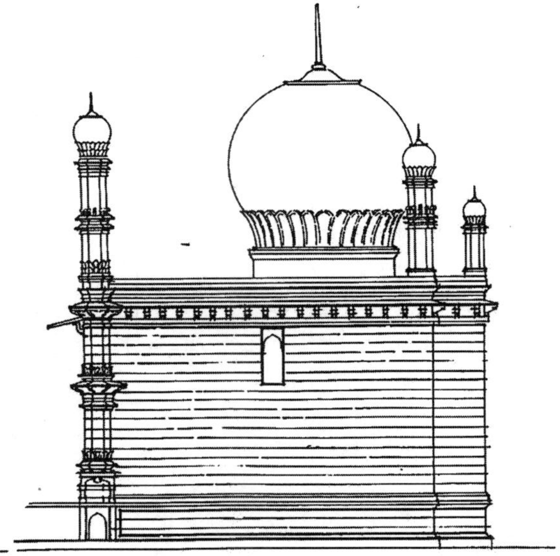

SIDE ELEVATION

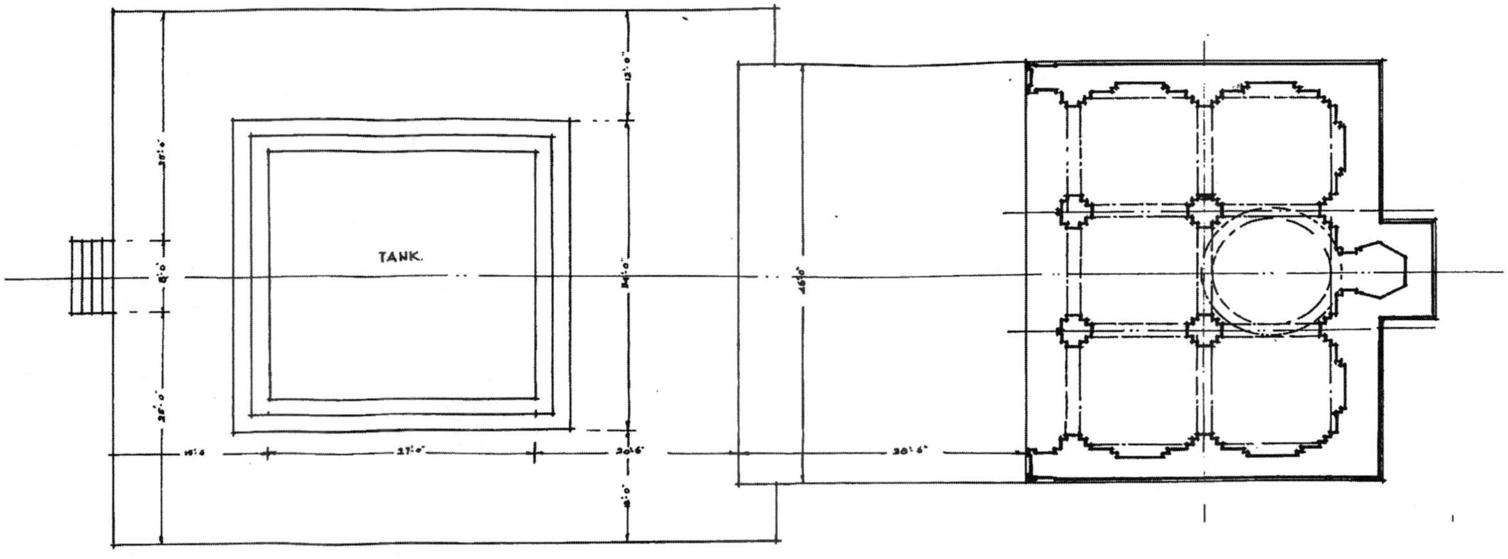

PLAN

MENS. & DELT. K.A. PARELKAR.

MENS. H.N. DALLAS.
DELT. J.VAZ.

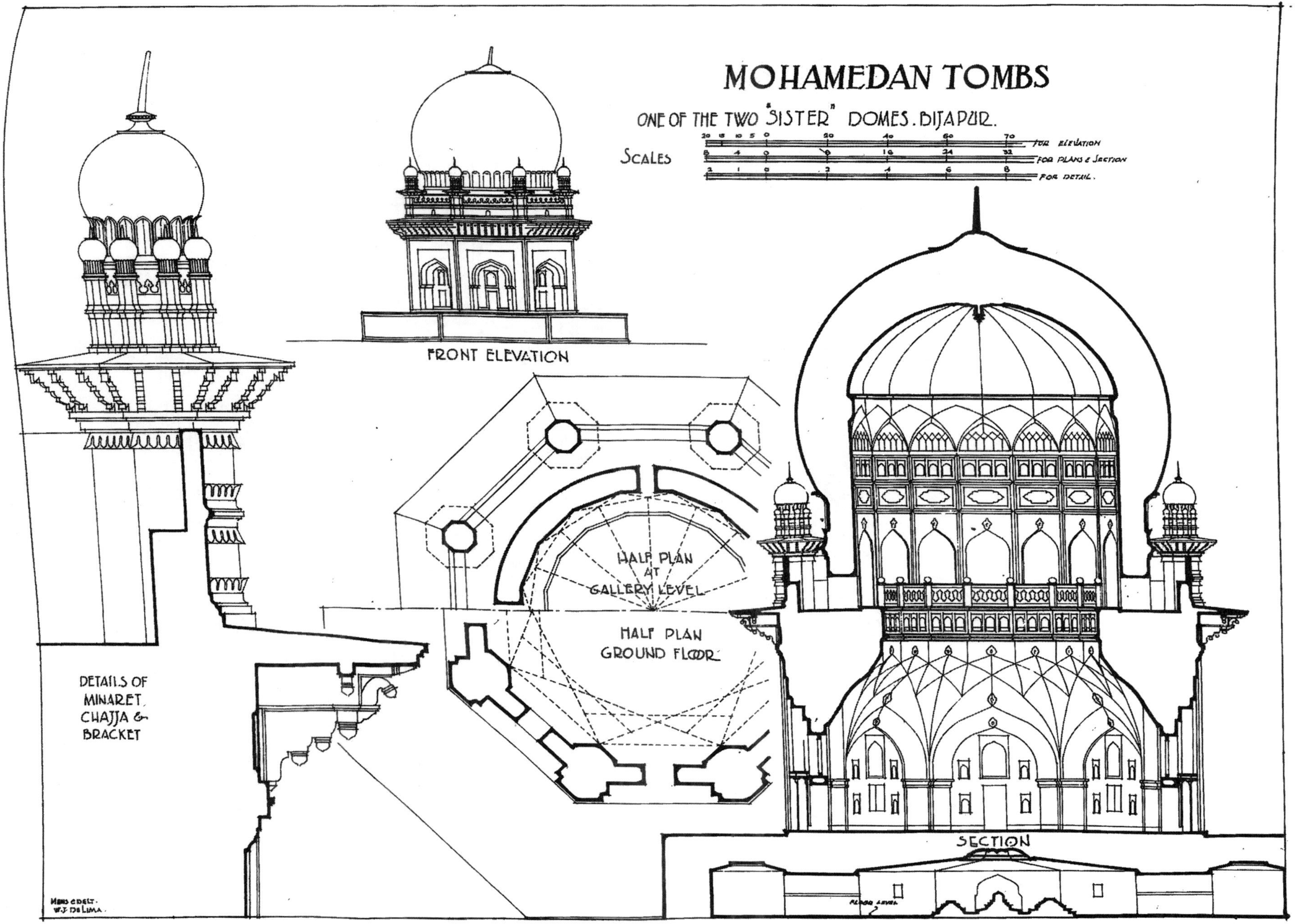
MOHAMEDAN TOMBS
ONE OF THE TWO "SISTER" DOMES. BIJAPUR.
SCALES
FOR ELEVATION
FOR PLANS & SECTION
FOR DETAIL.
FRONT ELEVATION
HALF PLAN AT GALLERY LEVEL
HALF PLAN GROUND FLOOR
SECTION
DETAILS OF MINARET, CHAJJA & BRACKET
MENS ET DELT.
W.J. DE LIMA.

AN INDIAN BALCONY (MOHAMEDAN)

FROM IBRAHIM ROZA BIJAPUR

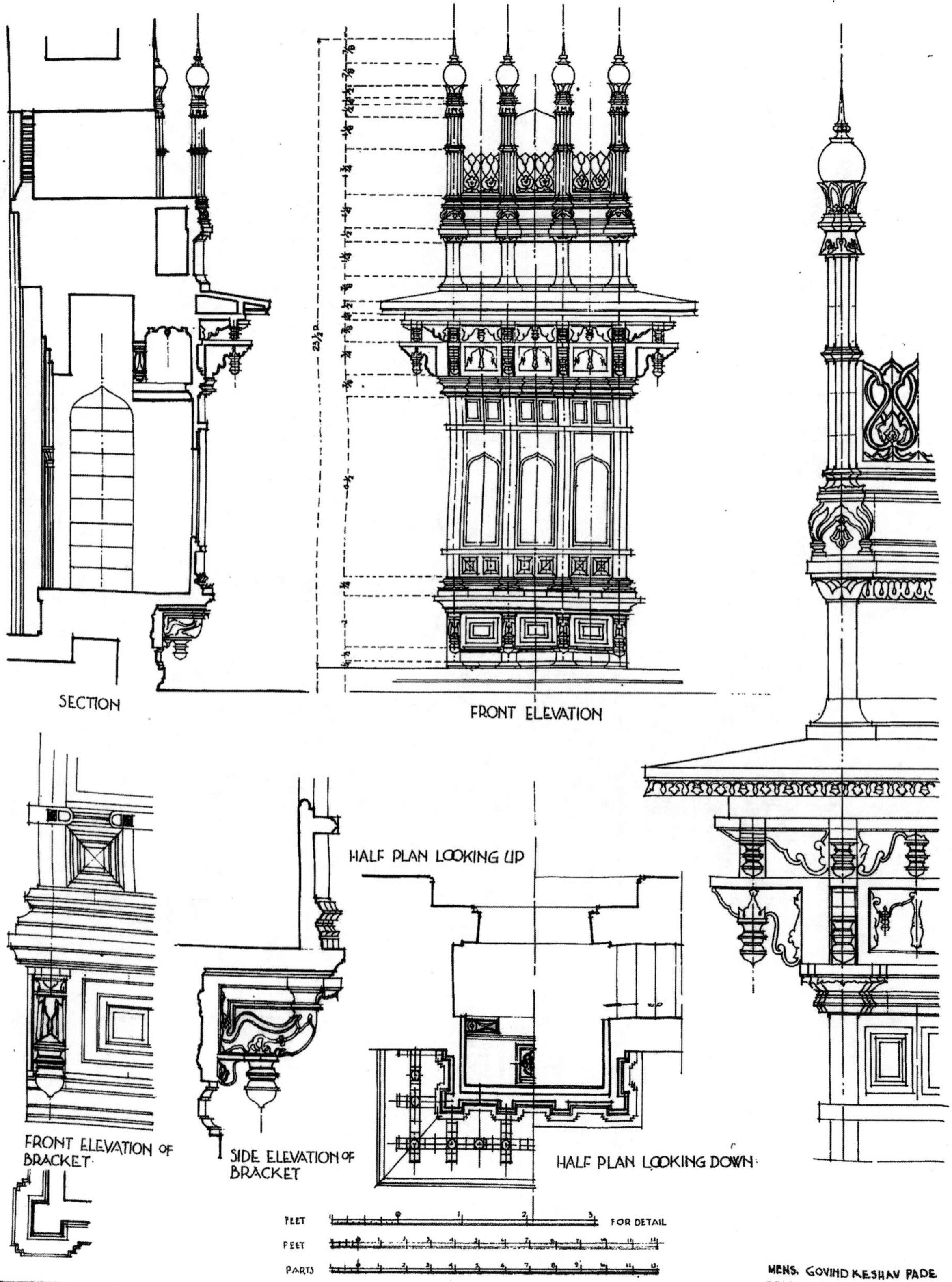

A MOHAMEDAN CEILING

FIRST FLOOR CEILING & INTERIOR - ELEVATION OF MEHTAR MAHAL. BIJAPUR.

CEILING PLAN

Scales.

FOR CEILING & ELEVATION

FOR SECTION

FOR DETAIL.

FIRST FLOOR INTERIOR ELEVATION

DETAIL IN CEILING

Mens. D.M. RUNGREY.
Delt. L.K. NANDWANA.

PLATE 32

PLAN LOOKING UP

STUCCO CEILING FROM THE CHHOTA ASAR, BIJAPUR

Scale 0 1 2 3 FEET

SECTION

MENS. & DELT. G.H. KARLEKAR.

A MOHAMEDAN CEILING

MOHAMEDAN PLASTER DETAIL

BEHRAM KHAN
KHAN-KHANA'S TOMB, BARA-PUL
OLD DELHI.

KEY PLAN
BERHAM KHAN-KHANA'S TOMB.

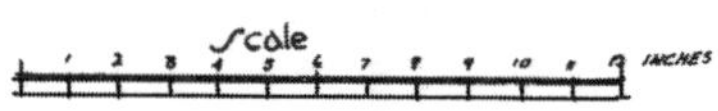

MENS. & DELT. S.D. CHITALIA.

HINDU HOUSE

RAJARAM RAO'S HOUSE. MADURA.

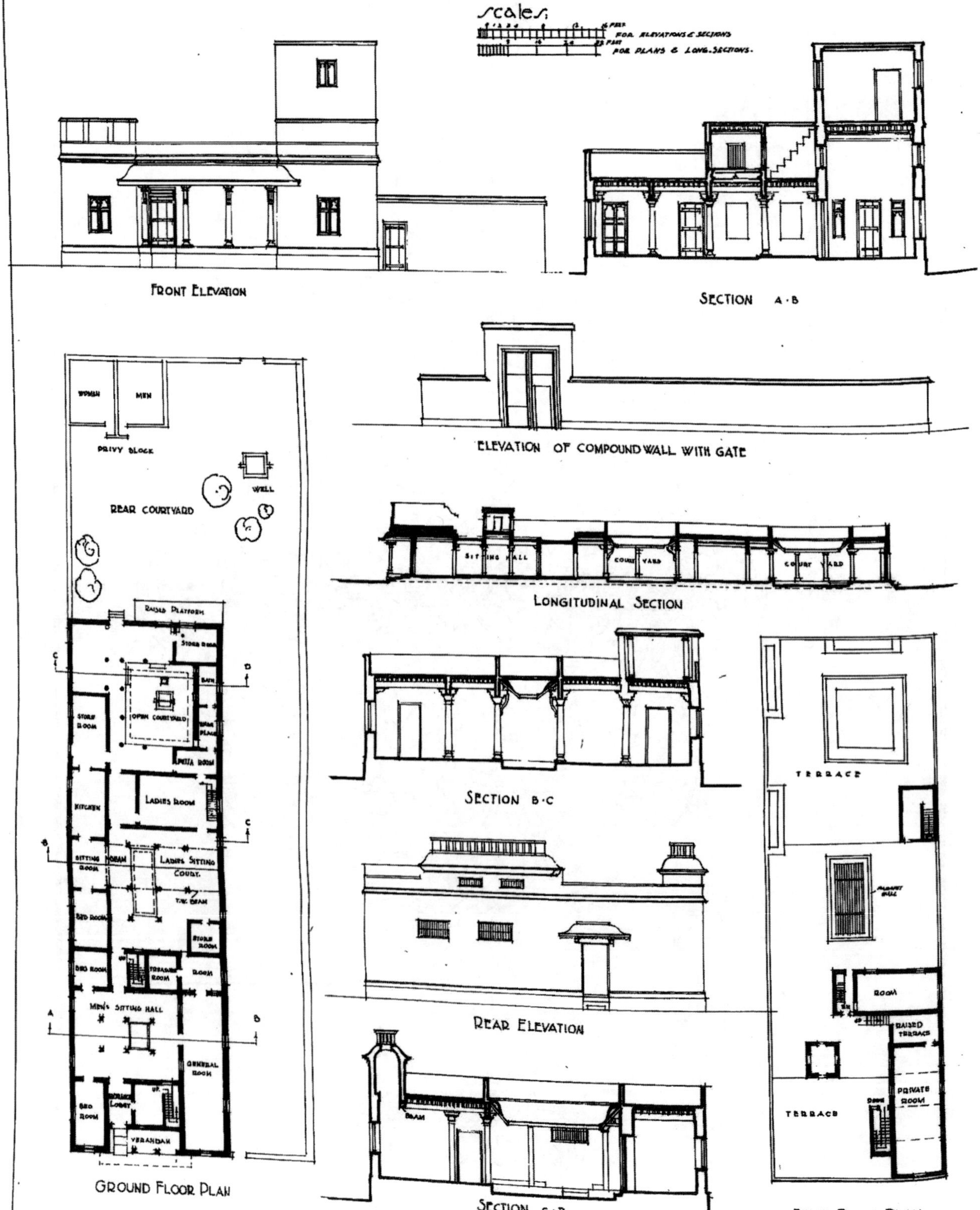

MENS. M.K. JADHAV.
DELT. M.K. JADHAV.

PLATE 55

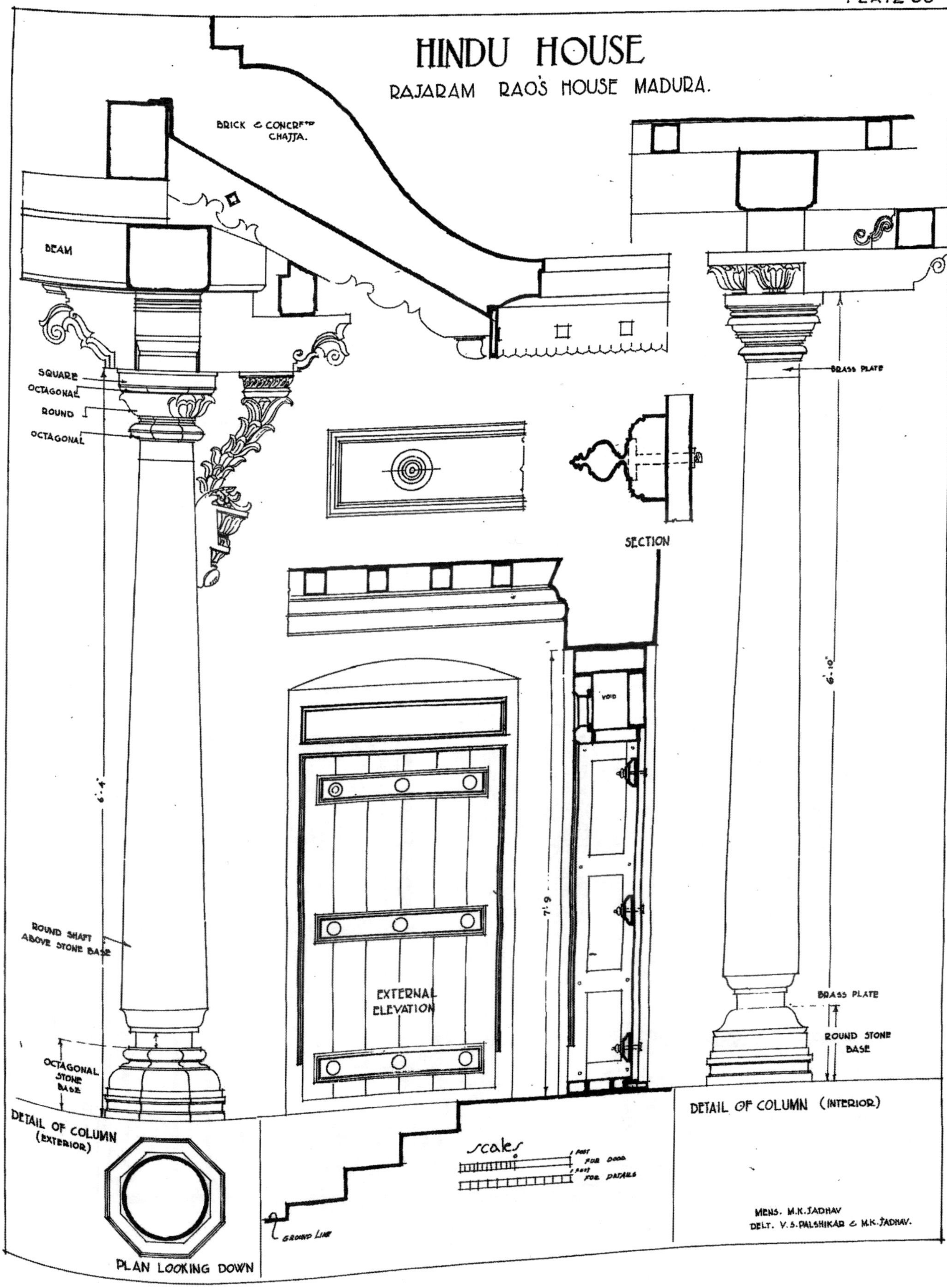
HINDU HOUSE
RAJARAM RAO'S HOUSE MADURA.
BRICK & CONCRETE CHAJJA.
BEAM
SQUARE
OCTAGONAL
ROUND
OCTAGONAL
BRASS PLATE
SECTION
VOID
6'-10"
6'-4"
7'-9"
ROUND SHAFT ABOVE STONE BASE
EXTERNAL ELEVATION
BRASS PLATE
ROUND STONE BASE
OCTAGONAL STONE BASE
DETAIL OF COLUMN (EXTERIOR)
DETAIL OF COLUMN (INTERIOR)
scales
FOR DOOR
FOR DETAILS
GROUND LINE
MENS. M.K. JADHAV
DELT. V.S. PALSHIKAR & M.K. JADHAV.
PLAN LOOKING DOWN

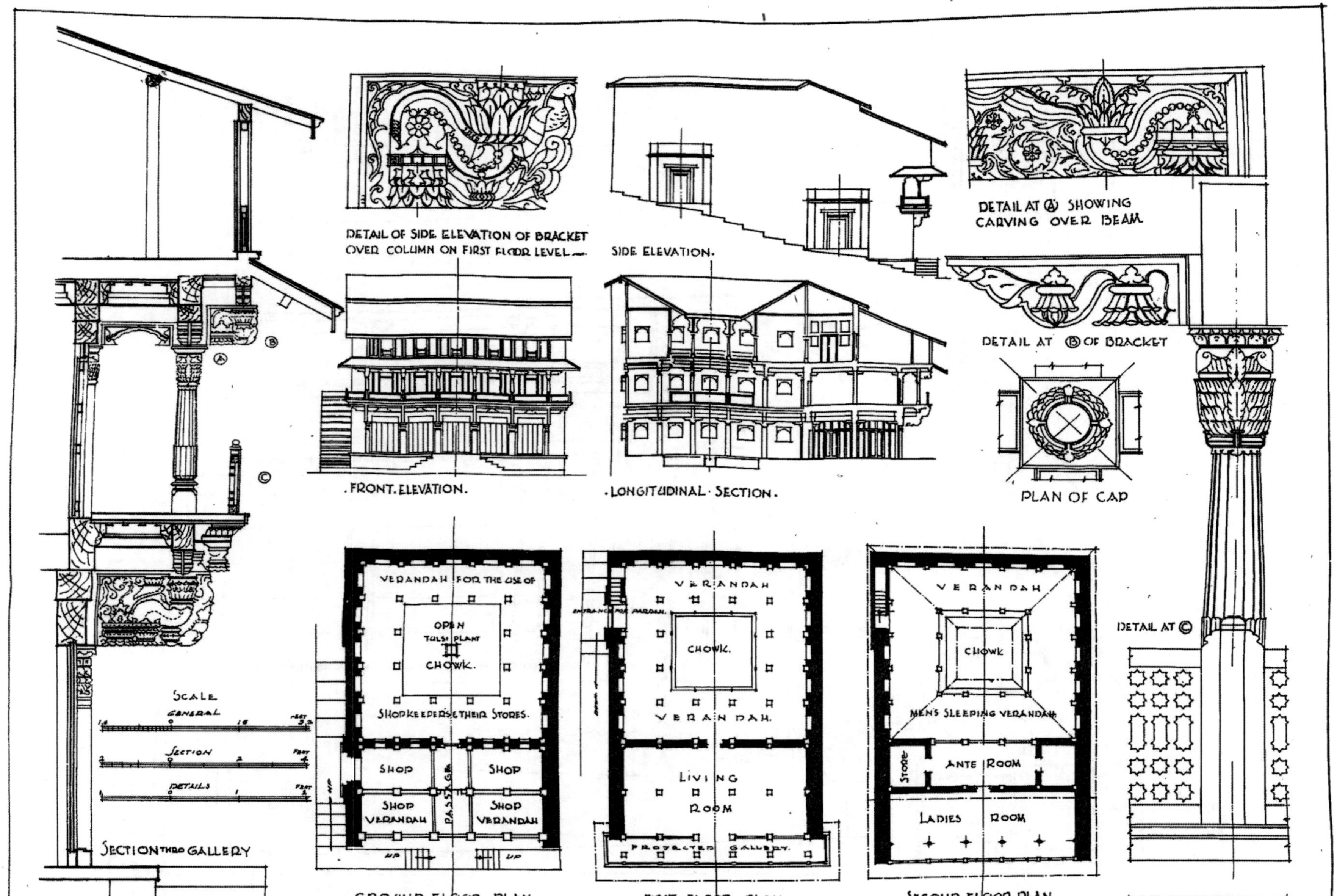

A HINDU HOUSE

INDIAN DOMESTIC WORK JATHARS. WADA AT NASIK.

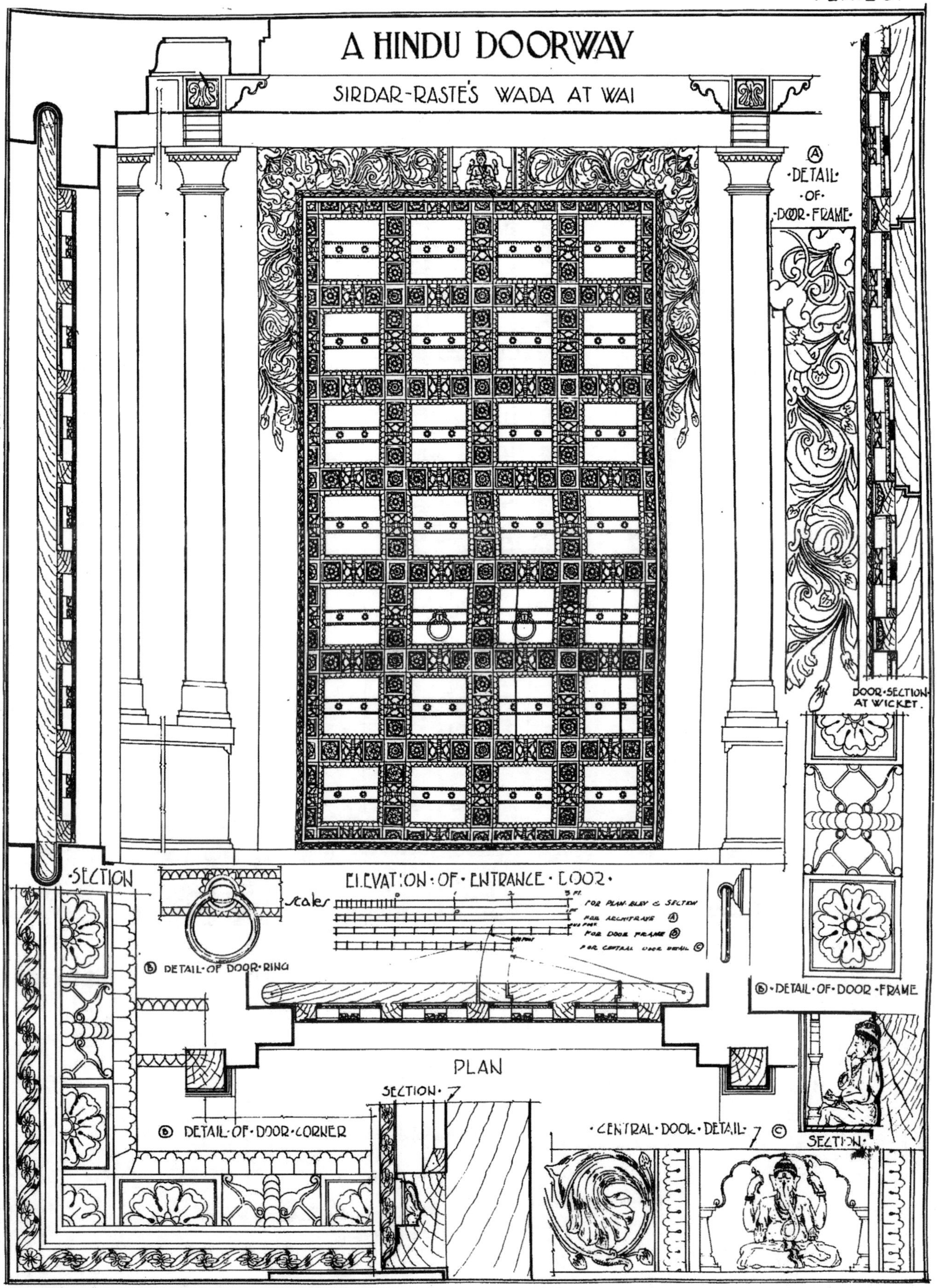

MENS & DELT. V.G.KALEKAR

A HINDU HOUSE

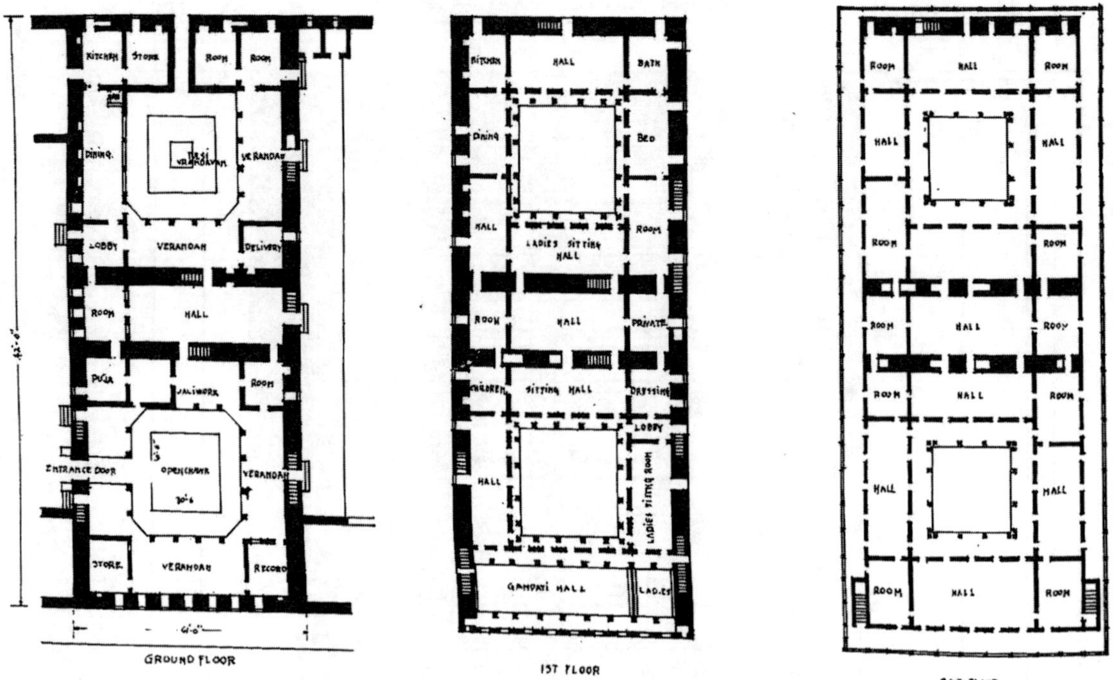

BHASKARRAO VITHAL'S WADA, BARODA.

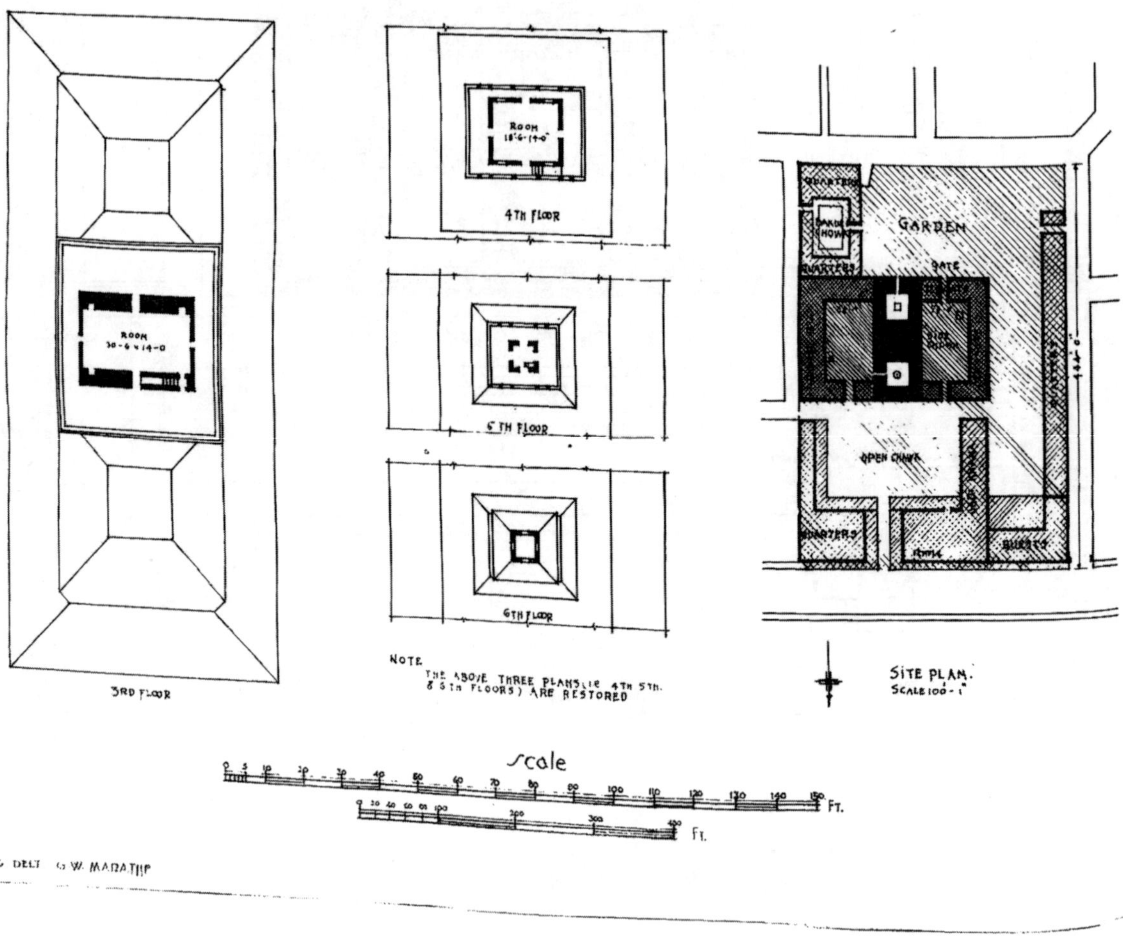

MEHTA G. DELT. G.W. MARATHE

A HINDU HOUSE

BHASKARRAO VITHAL'S WADA, BARODA.

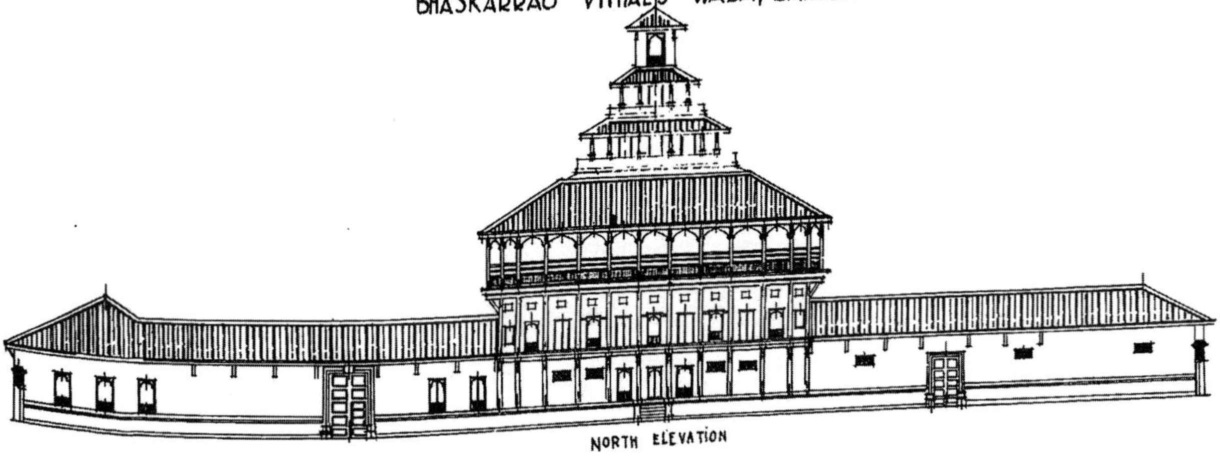

NORTH ELEVATION

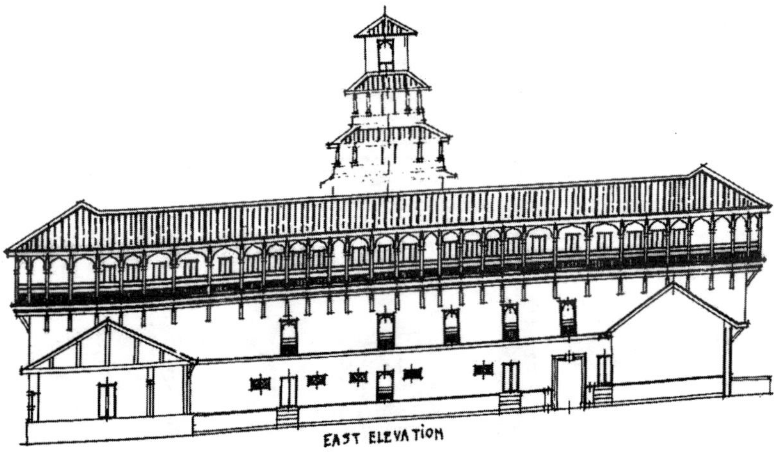

EAST ELEVATION

LONGITUDINAL SECTION

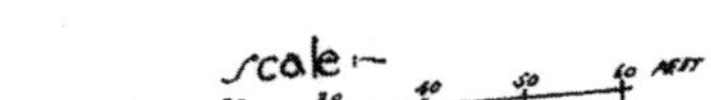

Meas & Delt. G.W. MARATHE

MENS & DELT. V.G. KALEKAR.

PLATE 41

HINDU PALACE

PALACE OF CHIEF AT BHOR STATE . NEAR POONA.

MEHS & DGLT · V. G. KALEKAR

HINDU HOUSE

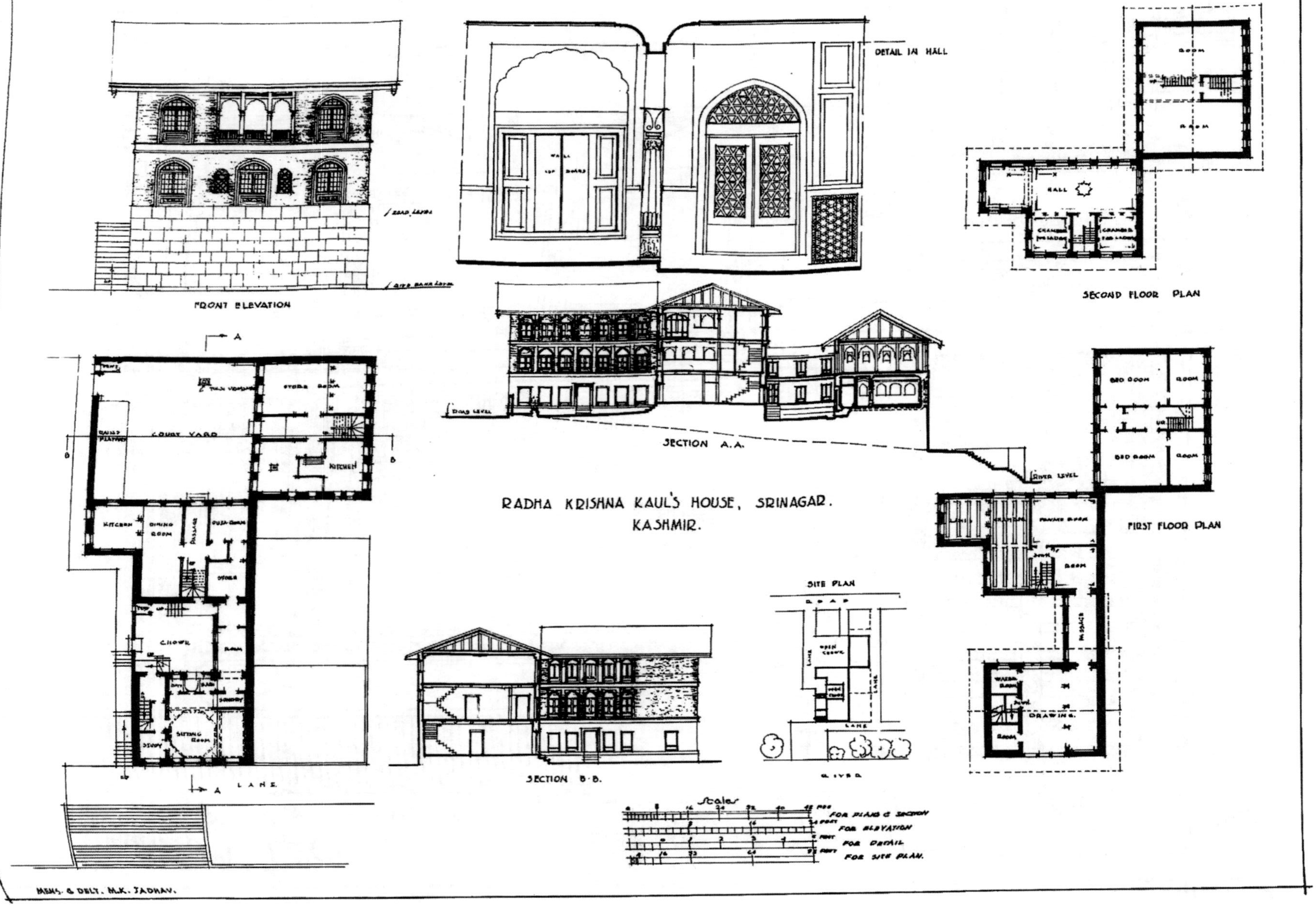
FRONT ELEVATION
DETAIL IN HALL
SECOND FLOOR PLAN
SECTION A.A.
FIRST FLOOR PLAN
RADHA KRISHNA KAUL'S HOUSE, SRINAGAR.
KASHMIR.
SITE PLAN
SECTION B-B.
COURT YARD
KITCHEN
CHOWK
SITTING ROOM
STUDY
DRAWING
BED ROOM
ROOM
HALL
LANE
ROAD LEVEL
RIVER LEVEL
Scales
FOR PLANS & SECTION
FOR ELEVATION
FOR DETAIL
FOR SITE PLAN.
MEAS. & DELT. M.K. JADHAV.

HINDU HOUSE
SECTION
ELEVATION OF TEAK SCREEN TO LADIES CHAMBER
Ⓐ DETAIL OF CEILING DECORATION
Ⓑ DETAILS OF CARVED PANELS TO WINDOW
Ⓒ DETAIL OF ENTRANCE DOOR
Ⓓ DETAIL OF ORNAMENT OVER ENTRANCE DOOR
RADHA KRISHNA KAUL'S
HOUSE
SRINAGAR, KASHMIR.
scales
FOR SCREEN
FOR DETAIL Ⓐ
FOR Ⓑ
FOR Ⓒ
FOR DETAIL Ⓓ
MEAS. M.K. JADHAV.
DELT. M.K. JADHAV.

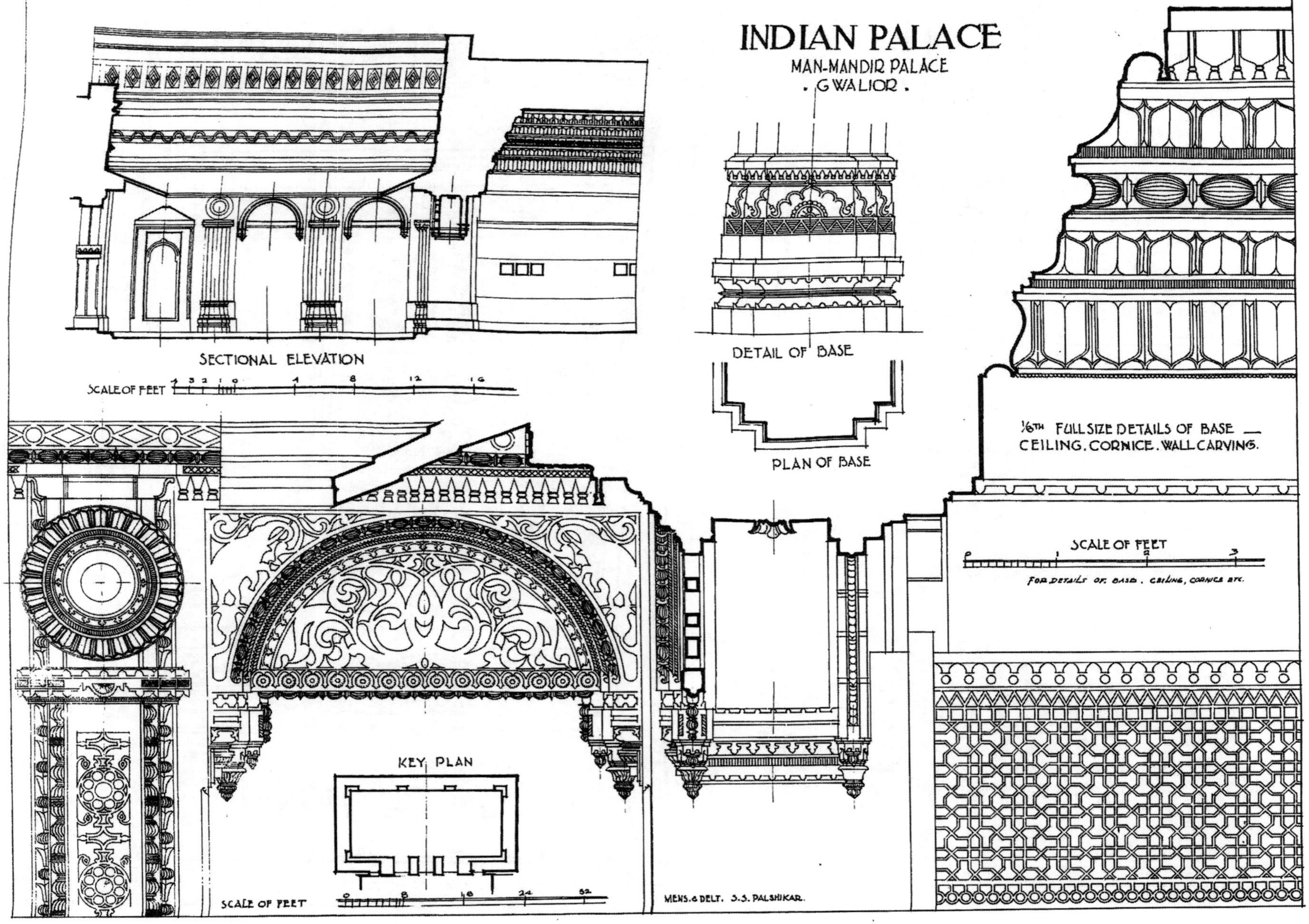
INDIAN PALACE
MAN-MANDIR PALACE
. GWALIOR .
SECTIONAL ELEVATION
SCALE OF FEET 4 3 2 1 0 4 8 12 16
DETAIL OF BASE
PLAN OF BASE
1/6TH FULL SIZE DETAILS OF BASE —
CEILING. CORNICE. WALL CARVING.
SCALE OF FEET 0 1 2 3
FOR DETAILS OF BASE . CEILING, CORNICE ETC.
KEY PLAN
SCALE OF FEET 0 8 16 24 32
MENS. & DELT. S.S. PALSHIKAR.

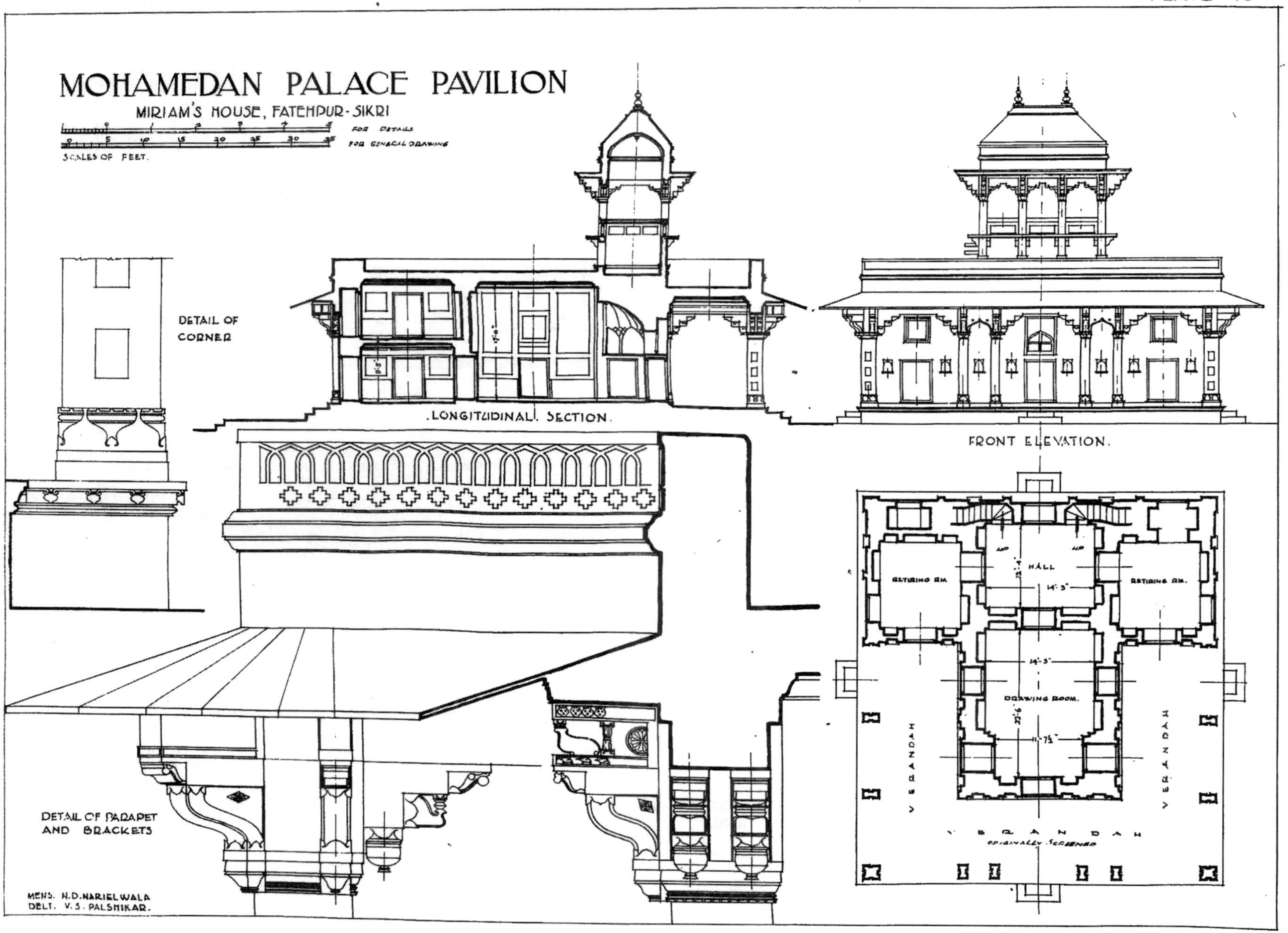
MOHAMEDAN PALACE PAVILION
MIRIAM'S HOUSE, FATEHPUR-SIKRI
FOR DETAILS
FOR GENERAL DRAWING
SCALES OF FEET.
DETAIL OF CORNER
.LONGITUDINAL. SECTION.
FRONT ELEVATION.
HALL
RETIRING RM.
RETIRING RM.
DRAWING ROOM.
VERANDAH
VERANDAH
VERANDAH
ORIGINALLY SCREENED
DETAIL OF PARAPET AND BRACKETS
MENS. N.D.NARIELWALA
DELT. V.S. PALSHIKAR.

PLATE 46

MOHAMEDAN PALACE PAVILION

RAJA BIRBAL'S HOUSE, AT FATHEPUR-SIKRI.

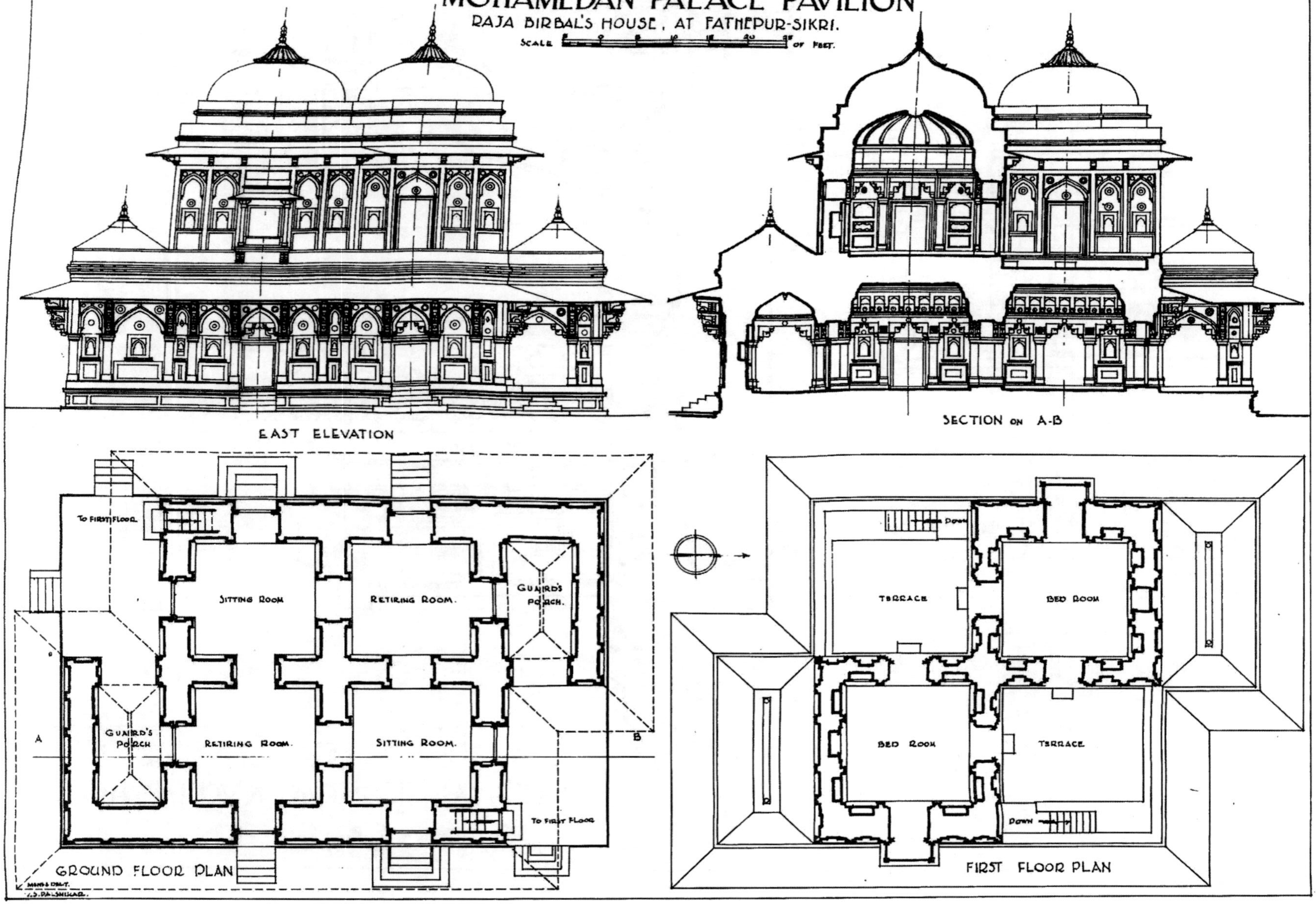

MOHAMEDAN PANELLING

RAJA BIRBAL'S HOUSE, FATEHPUR-SIKRI.

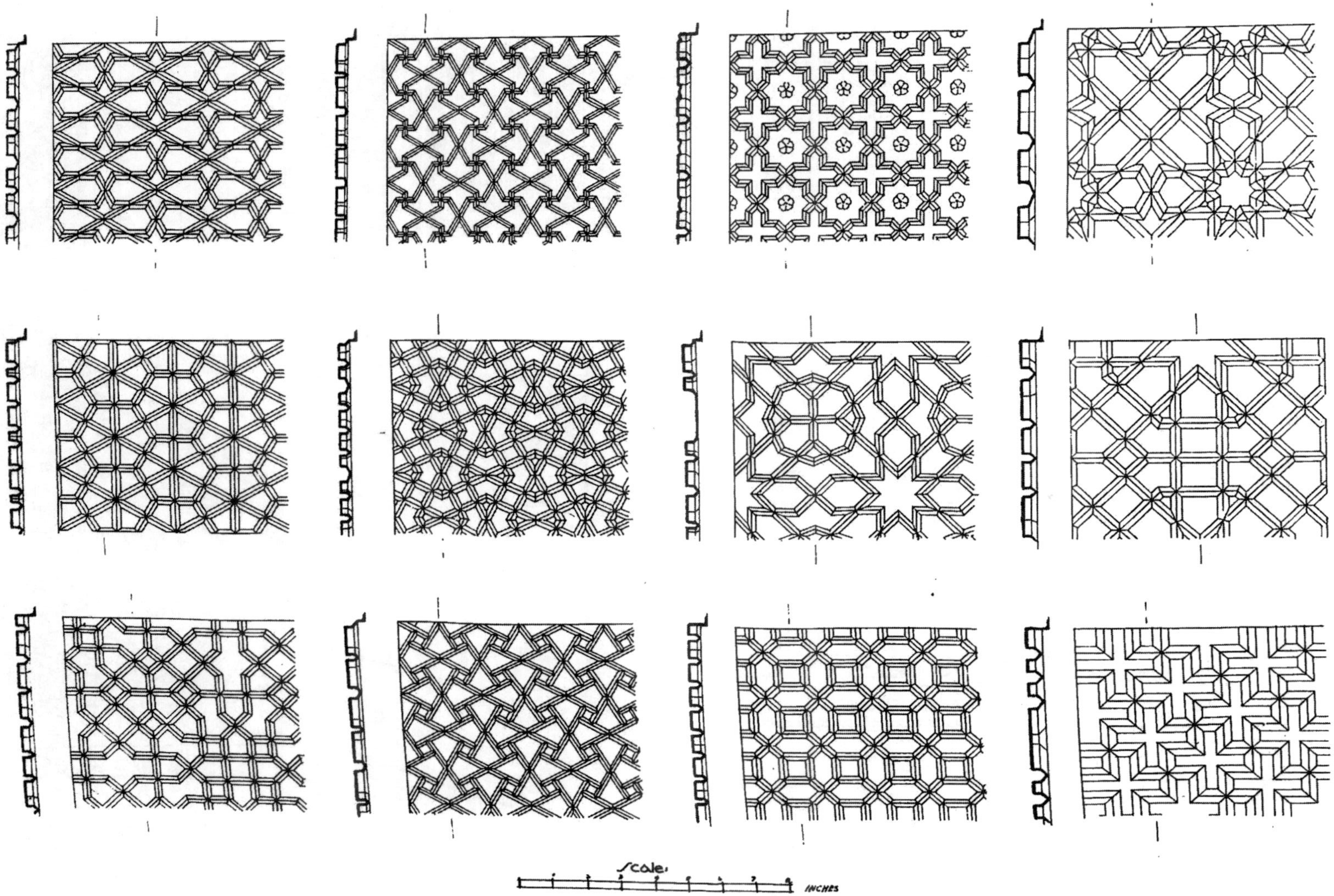

MENS. ARCH. SURVEY.
DELT. S. B. UMRIGAR.

MOHAMEDAN PALACE PAVILION

TURKISH SULTANA'S HOUSE, FATEHPUR-SIKRI.

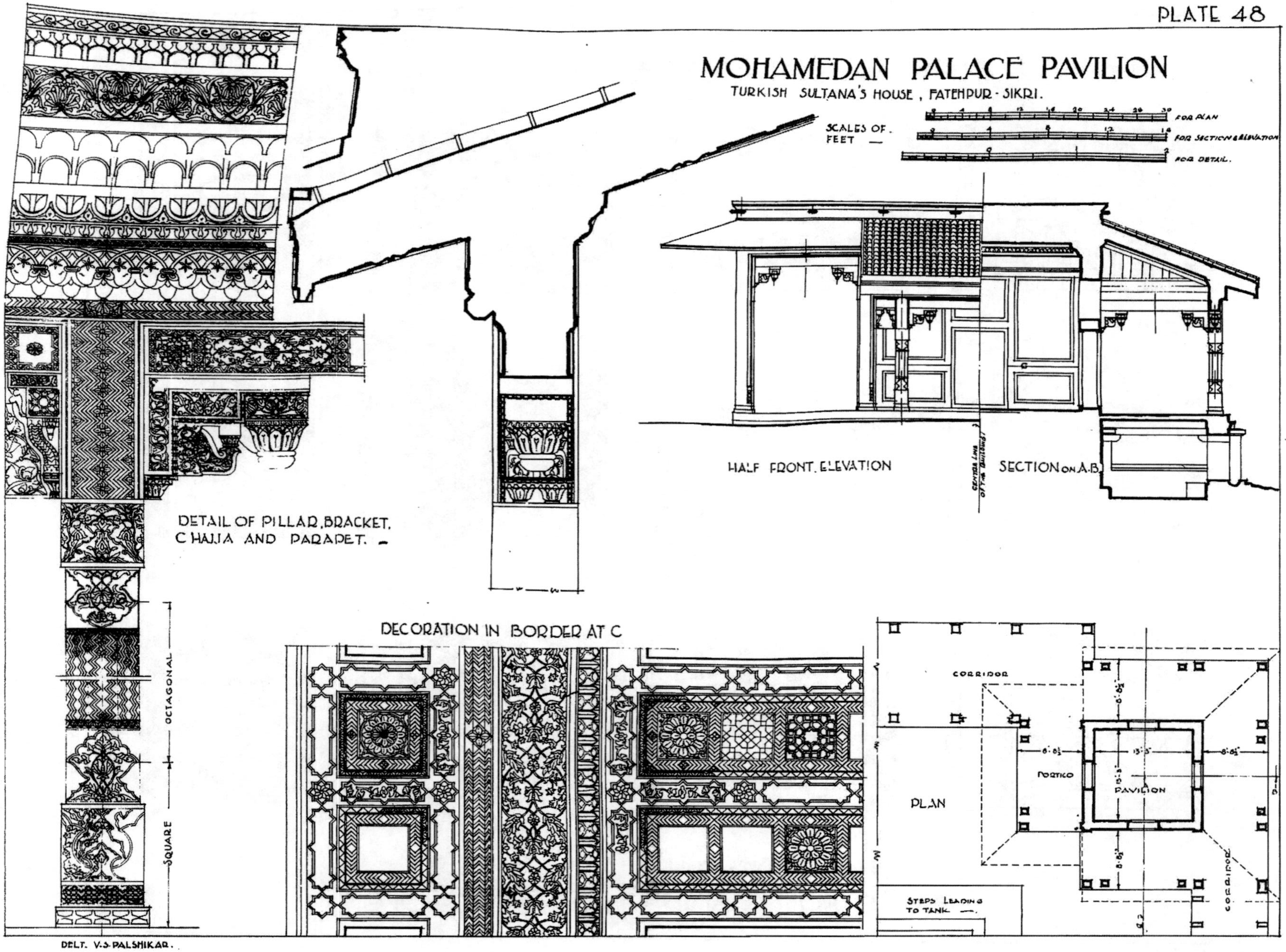

A MOHAMEDAN ARCADED GALLERY

LADIES GALLERY OVERLOOKING PALACE BAZAAR, AT AGRA.

MENS & DELT. S.M. KADRI

INDIAN PALACE GATE-WAY.

UDAIPUR.

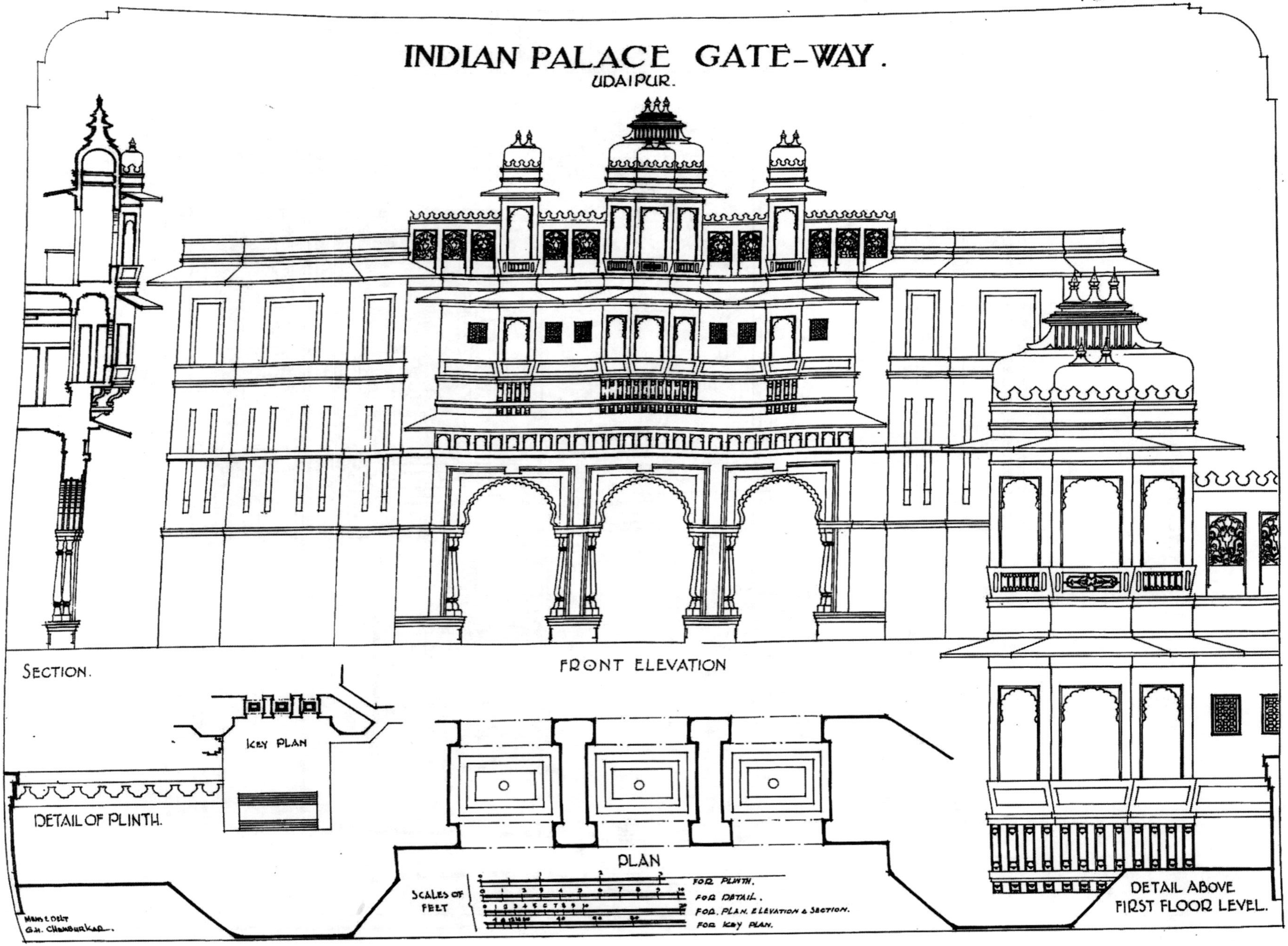

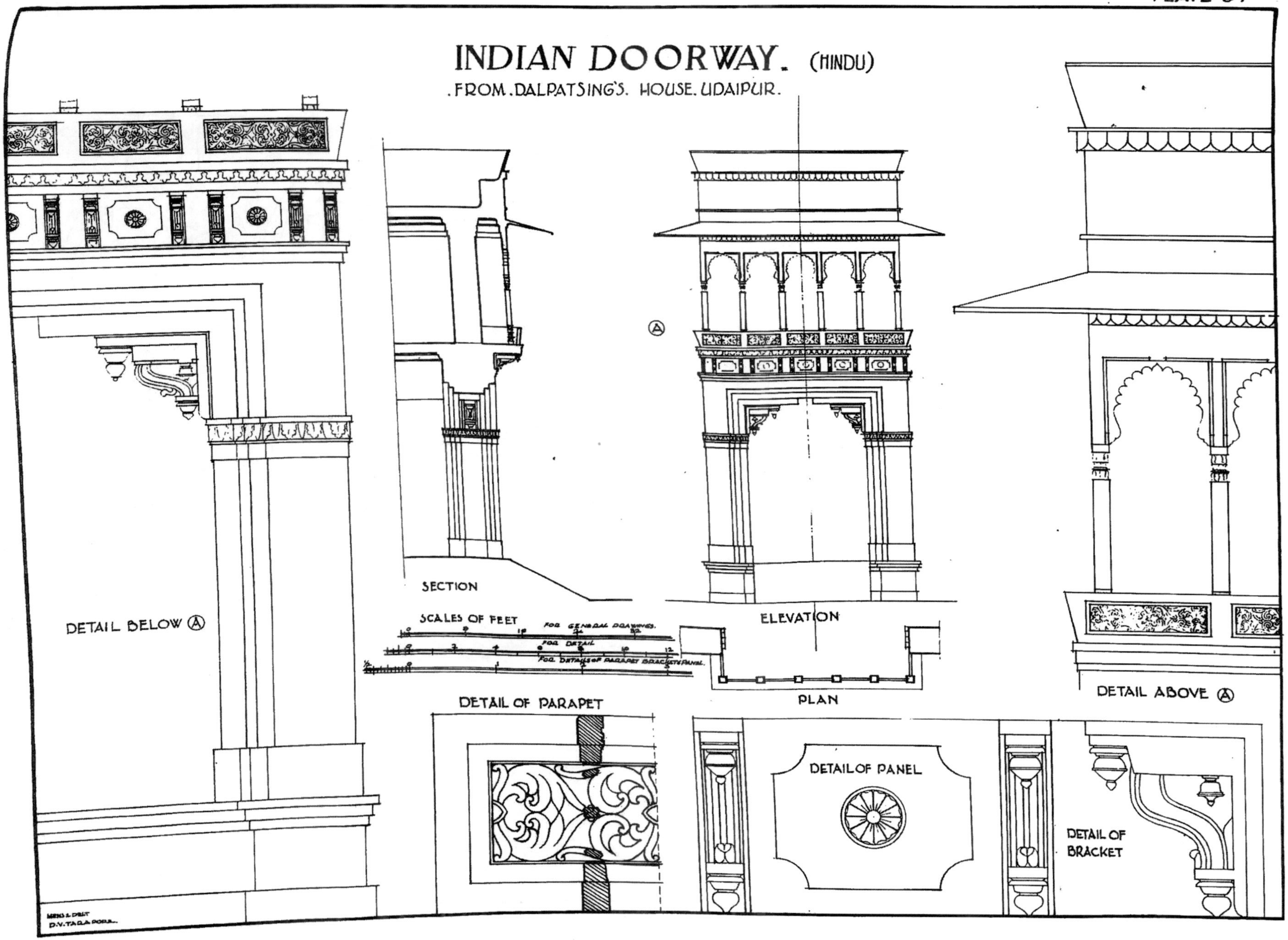
INDIAN DOORWAY. (HINDU)
.FROM.DALPATSING'S. HOUSE. UDAIPUR.
SECTION
ELEVATION
PLAN
DETAIL BELOW Ⓐ
DETAIL ABOVE Ⓐ
SCALES OF FEET
FOR GENERAL DRAWINGS.
FOR DETAIL
FOR DETAILS OF PARAPET BRACKET & PANEL.
DETAIL OF PARAPET
DETAIL OF PANEL
DETAIL OF BRACKET
MENS & DELT
D.V. TARAPORA.

HINDU JALIS

FROM THE PALACE AT GAN-GHORE GHAT, PICHOLA LAKE, UDAIPUR.

MENS. D.S. POWALE
DELT. L.K. NANDWANA.